The Books of Baruch & The Exiles

The Secret Writings of the Prophet Baruch and the Future of Israel

A Modern Translation

Adapted for the Contemporary Reader

Various Ancient Writers
(Attributed to Baruch and Jeremiah)

Translated by Tim Zengerink

© **Copyright 2025**
All rights reserved.

It is not legal to reproduce, duplicate, or transmit any part of this document in either electronic means or in printed format. Recording of this publication is strictly prohibited and any storage of this document is not allowed unless with written permission from the publisher except for the use of brief quotations in a book review.

This book contains works of fiction. Any resemblance to persons living or dead, or places, events, or locations is purely coincidental.

Table of Contents

Preface - Message to the Reader 1

Introduction 4

The Letter of Jeremiah 9

    Introduction 9
    The Letter of Jeremiah 9

The Book of Baruch 15

    Introduction to the Book of Baruch 15
    Chapter 1 16
    Chapter 2 17
    Chapter 3 20
    Chapter 4 22
    Chapter 5 24

The Apocalypse of Baruch 26

    Chapter 1~5 26
    Chapter 6~9 28
    Chapter 10~12 30
    Chapter 13~15 33
    Chapter 16~20 35
    Chapter 21 37
    Chapter 22~30 39
    Chapter 31~34 43
    Chapter 35~43 45
    Chapter 44~47 50
    Chapter 48~52 52

Chapter 53~54 58

Chapter 55~68 61

Chapter 69~76 68

Chapter 77 73

Chapter 78~81 76

Chapter 82~84 78

Chapter 85~87 83

The Third Book of Baruch 86

Chapter One 86

Chapter Two 87

Chapter Three 88

Chapter Four 89

Chapter Five 93

Chapter Six 93

Chapter Seven 95

Chapter Eight 96

Chapter Nine 97

Chapter Ten 98

Chapter Eleven 99

Chapter Twelve 100

Chapter Thirteen 100

Chapter Fourteen 101

Chapter Fifteen 101

Chapter Sixteen 102

Chapter Seventeen 103

Thank You for Reading 104

Preface - Message to the Reader

What If You Could Help Rebuild the Greatest Library in Human History?

Thousands of years ago, the Library of Alexandria stood as the crown jewel of human achievement — a sanctuary where the collected wisdom of every known civilization was gathered, preserved, and shared freely.

And then, it was lost.

Through fire, conquest, and the slow erosion of time, humanity lost not just books — but ideas, dreams, discoveries, and stories that could have changed the world forever.

Today, the Library of Alexandria lives again — and you are invited to be a part of its restoration.

Our mission is simple yet profound:

To rebuild the greatest library the world has ever known, and to translate all timeless works into every language and dialect, so that no seeker of knowledge is ever left behind again.

By joining our movement to rebuild the modern Library of Alexandria, you become part of an unprecedented mission:

- **Unlimited Access to the Greatest Audiobooks & eBooks Ever Written:**

    Instantly explore thousands of legendary works—Plato, Shakespeare, Jane Austen, Leo Tolstoy, and countless more. All instantly available to read or listen, placing a complete literary universe at your fingertips.

- **Beautiful Paperback & Deluxe Editions at Printing Cost**

  Own any title as an elegant paperback, deluxe hardcover, or stunning collectible boxset—offered to you at true printing cost, delivered straight to your door. Build your personal Library of Alexandria, crafted for beauty, built for durability, and worthy of proud display.

- **Fresh Translations for Modern Readers—in Every Language & Dialect**

  Enjoy timeless masterpieces reimagined in clear, contemporary language—no more outdated phrases or obscure references. Alongside the original versions, we're tirelessly translating these classics into every language and dialect imaginable, ensuring accessibility and understanding across cultures and generations.

- **Join a Global Renaissance of Literature & Knowledge**

  You directly support expanding our library, publishing deluxe editions at true cost, translating works into all global languages, and bringing humanity's greatest stories to people everywhere. By joining today, you're not just preserving a legacy of masterpieces; you set in motion a powerful wave of literary accessibility.

Become a Torchbearer of Knowledge.

Join us for free now at **LibraryofAlexandria.com**

Together, we will ensure that the light of human wisdom never fades again.

With gratitude and a shared love of knowledge,
The Modern Library of Alexandria Team

Visit:

www.libraryofalexandria.com

Or scan the code below:

Introduction

Baruch's Voice in the Shadows of Destruction

In the long history of sacred literature, few figures occupy as poignant a position as Baruch, the faithful scribe of the prophet Jeremiah. While Jeremiah thundered warnings and lamented openly for the fall of Judah, it was Baruch who recorded, remembered, and reflected. He was both witness and chronicler to one of the greatest national traumas in Jewish history—the fall of Jerusalem to Babylon in 586 BCE. The destruction of the Temple, the shattering of the Davidic kingdom, and the forced exile of its people marked a moment of loss that seemed to fracture the very covenant between God and Israel.

Yet, it is precisely in this darkness that Baruch's writings shine. For in them, we hear not only mourning and judgment, but hope. Not just condemnation, but redemption. The writings attributed to Baruch—spread across several distinct texts—are unified by a single theme: the belief that beyond punishment lies promise, beyond suffering lies salvation. These books are not simply historical or prophetic; they are deeply theological, emotional, and spiritual. They offer readers a vision of how to endure exile, how to return to God in times of judgment, and how to maintain hope when the world seems forsaken.

The Books of Baruch & The Exiles gathers four key texts: the canonical Book of Baruch, the apocalyptic Apocalypse of Baruch, the visionary Third Book of Baruch, and the often-overlooked Letter of Jeremiah. Together, they form a literary and spiritual journey from the ruins of Jerusalem to the mysteries of heaven itself.

The Book of Baruch:
Lamentation, Confession, and Covenant

The Book of Baruch opens with sorrow but quickly turns toward repentance. Set in the immediate aftermath of Jerusalem's fall, it presents a community seeking to understand its suffering and return to covenantal faithfulness. The first part is a national confession—a recognition that Israel's downfall was not arbitrary but the result of long-standing disobedience.

This confession is followed by beautiful prayers and poetic reflections on wisdom, justice, and divine mercy. One of the most powerful themes is the accessibility of wisdom to all who seek it—not through lineage or location, but through humility and obedience. Baruch reaffirms God's enduring covenant with Israel and urges the people not to despair, but to remember that exile is not the end of the story.

In this book, Baruch acts as both prophet and priest—leading the people in prayer, encouraging repentance, and offering reassurance that the God who judged will also restore.

The Apocalypse of Baruch:
Visions of Judgment and Restoration

Also known as 2 Baruch, this extensive text offers a deeply apocalyptic perspective. Composed after the destruction of the Second Temple in 70 CE, it is often viewed as a response to that second catastrophe, projected back onto the memory of the first exile. It takes the form of divine dialogues, angelic visions, and end-time revelations.

Baruch, now portrayed as a visionary, is shown the future of Israel, the fate of the righteous and the wicked, and the structure of divine justice. He struggles with the same questions that haunt every generation of faithful believers: Why does the righteous suffer? How can a just God allow evil to triumph? What is the meaning of history? What hope remains for the covenant people?

God's response is both sobering and comforting. Baruch is told that history follows a divine pattern, and that though the wicked may prosper now, their triumph is fleeting. The righteous, on the other hand, are promised future vindication, resurrection, and participation in the world to come. The text also introduces eschatological images of the Messiah, cosmic upheaval, and divine judgment, making it a precursor to later Christian apocalyptic literature.

Through The Apocalypse of Baruch, we see a deepening of the theological imagination—one that seeks meaning in catastrophe and dares to proclaim hope in the face of despair.

The Third Book of Baruch: Mystical Ascent and Cosmic Secrets

The Third Book of Baruch (3 Baruch) is a departure in tone and style from the other Baruch texts. It is a mystical and visionary work, likely composed in the early centuries of the Common Era, and it focuses on Baruch's ascent through the heavens. Guided by an angel, Baruch is shown the mysteries of the cosmos: the movements of the sun and moon, the punishment of the fallen angels, and the hidden architecture of divine creation.

This text is less concerned with history and more with metaphysics and spiritual vision. It seeks to explain not just what happened to Israel, but how the universe is ordered, and what role humans play within it. The fall of Jerusalem is implicitly a part of this order, a result of the spiritual corruption that distorts the harmony of creation.

Baruch's journey is both literal and symbolic. As he ascends, he gains deeper insight into divine justice, the nature of angels and demons, and the eternal purpose of God. 3 Baruch is part of a broader tradition of Jewish apocalyptic ascent literature, linking it to other texts like 1 Enoch and the later Hekhalot writings.

For modern readers, this book may appear otherworldly or esoteric, but its message remains powerful: spiritual vision is essential in times of crisis, and divine mysteries continue to unfold even when earthly structures collapse.

The Letter of Jeremiah: A Prophetic Warning Against Idolatry

Often included as the final chapter of Baruch or standing on its own, the Letter of Jeremiah is a sharp and prophetic polemic against idolatry. Framed as a message from Jeremiah to the exiles in Babylon, it warns the people not to be seduced by the gods of the nations, whose idols are powerless, blind, and mute.

This letter emphasizes a core biblical theme: the uniqueness of the one true God. Its rhetorical style is biting, sarcastic, and urgent. The exiles are reminded that while they may be far from Jerusalem, they are not far from God—so long as they remain faithful. The message is one of spiritual resistance: do not assimilate, do not compromise, do not forget who you are.

This short but potent text resonates strongly today, reminding readers of the dangers of modern idolatry—be it materialism, nationalism, or any form of misplaced worship. It pairs perfectly with the other Baruch texts as a final exhortation to remain rooted in truth, even in the land of exile.

Restoration Through Revelation

What unites all these writings—despite their differences in form and tone—is their deep concern with faith in the face of loss. The Books of Baruch are texts of exile, but they are also texts of return—not just to a homeland, but to God. They teach that while history may break the body, it need not break the soul. That judgment, rightly understood, is an invitation to transformation. That hope, no matter how buried, can rise anew.

In these writings, Baruch emerges as one of the great forgotten voices of sacred tradition. He is not just Jeremiah's scribe—he is a prophet in his own right. He laments like David, intercedes like Moses, and envisions like Daniel. His words speak across centuries to anyone who has suffered loss, witnessed injustice, or waited on a promise not yet fulfilled.

This modern translation brings these ancient voices into today's world, with clarity, reverence, and insight. Archaic phrasing has been refreshed, while preserving the poetic cadence and spiritual intensity of the originals. Contextual notes help guide the reader through the more complex passages, and each text is framed to highlight its significance.

Whether you are approaching these writings as historical documents, theological reflections, or spiritual meditations, they will reward your reading with wisdom, perspective, and profound insight.

May these forgotten prophecies guide your path through the ruins and into the light.

The Letter of Jeremiah

Introduction

This letter, believed to be from the prophet Jeremiah, was sent to the Israelites living in exile in Babylon. It warns them to stay faithful to God and not be fooled by idols. These statues, made of wood, silver, and gold, cannot see, move, or do anything. The letter strongly criticizes idol worship and uses clear examples to show that these false gods have no real power. It reminds the exiles that only the one true God controls history, nature, and their future.

The Letter of Jeremiah

This is a copy of a letter that Jeremiah wrote to the people who were being taken to Babylon as captives by the king. The letter contained a message from God that he was told to share with them.

The People Will Be Captives for A Long Time

Because you have disobeyed God, King Nebuchadnezzar of Babylon will take you away as captives. When you arrive in Babylon, you will have to stay there for a very long time—up to seven generations. But after that, I will bring you back home safely.

While you are in Babylon, you will see statues made of silver, gold, and wood. People carry them around, and many nations are afraid of them. Do not follow their customs or let fear of their gods take over your heart. Even if you see large crowds worshiping these idols, stay strong and remember:

"Only the Lord is worthy of our worship."

My angel will be with you, protecting you and watching over your lives.

The Powerlessness of Idols

Carpenters shape their tongues, and they are covered with gold and silver, but they are not real and cannot speak. People take gold and make crowns for their statues, just like they would for a young woman who loves jewelry.

Sometimes, priests secretly take gold and silver from these idols and use it for themselves. Some even give it to prostitutes on the rooftops. They dress these statues in fine clothing to make them look like people, but they are only made of silver, gold, and wood.

These idols cannot even protect themselves from rust and decay. When they are dressed in purple robes, their faces still get covered in thick dust from the temple, and someone has to clean them.

Some of these statues hold a staff like a judge, but they have no power to punish anyone. Others carry a dagger or an ax, but they cannot protect themselves from war or thieves.

This proves they are not gods—so do not be afraid of them.

The Worthlessness of Idols

Just like a broken dish is useless, these idols are also worthless, even when placed in temples. Their eyes get covered in dust from people walking by. The priests lock up the temples with doors, bars, and locks, not because the idols have power, but to keep thieves from stealing them.

More lamps are lit for these idols than for the people who worship them, yet the statues cannot see the light. They are no different from a wooden beam in a temple. Over time, insects and crawling creatures eat away at their clothing, but they do not notice. Their faces get covered in smoke from the temple, but they cannot clean themselves. Birds and bats rest on them, and even cats climb on their heads.

This should be enough proof that they are not gods—so do not be afraid of them.

The gold used to decorate them only shines when someone cleans it, and even when they were made, they felt nothing. People spend a lot of money on them, but they are lifeless. Since they have no feet, others must carry them, proving how powerless they are. Those who serve them will feel ashamed.

If one of these statues falls to the ground, someone has to pick it up. If it is knocked over, it cannot get back up by itself. People leave gifts in front of them, just as they would for the dead. The priests take the offerings and use the money for themselves. Their wives keep some of the sacrificed meat but do not share it with the poor or those in need. Some of these sacrifices are even handled by women during their monthly cycle or after giving birth—something that would normally be considered impure.

Knowing all this, you should realize that these idols are not gods—so do not fear them.

How can they be called gods? Women cook food for them as if they were people. In their temples, priests wear torn clothes, shave their heads and beards, and uncover their heads. They cry out and wail, just like mourners at a funeral. Some priests even take the clothes from these idols and use them for their wives and children.

If someone treats these idols well or badly, they cannot do anything in return. They have no power to make or remove a king. They cannot give riches, and they do not punish those who break promises to them. They cannot save anyone from death or protect the weak from the strong. They cannot heal the blind or help someone in trouble. They have no pity for widows and do nothing for orphans.

These statues, made of wood and covered in gold and silver, are no different from regular stones. People who worship them will end up feeling embarrassed. So why would anyone believe they are gods or call them that?

The Foolishness Of Worshiping Idols

Even the Chaldeans themselves do not respect their idols. When they see someone who cannot speak, they pray to Bel, hoping it will give the person a voice, as if the statue could understand. Yet, they fail to see how foolish this is. They continue worshiping these idols, even though they have no real power.

Women sit along the pathways with ropes around them, burning bran as incense. When one of them is chosen by a passerby and taken with him, she mocks the others who were not chosen, thinking she is more attractive. Everything done for these idols is meaningless. So why would anyone believe they are gods or call them that?

Carpenters and goldsmiths make these statues, shaping them however they want. The people who create them will not live forever, so how can something they make be a god? These idols leave behind nothing but lies and shame for those who follow them.

When war or disaster comes, the priests quickly discuss where they can hide themselves and their gods. How can anyone not see that these statues are powerless? They cannot even save themselves from destruction. Since they are only wood covered in gold and silver, one day it will be clear to everyone that they are not gods. The whole world will recognize that they are just man-made objects and have nothing to do with the true God. Who wouldn't realize they are fake?

They cannot appoint a king or send rain to the earth. They have no power to make judgments or defend someone who is wronged. They are as useless as crows flying between the sky and the ground. If a fire starts in a temple full of wooden idols, the priests will run to save themselves, but the statues will burn like ordinary wood. They cannot resist a king or an enemy. So why should anyone believe they are gods?

These idols cannot even protect themselves from thieves. Anyone who wants to can take their gold, silver, and fine robes, and they will not stop them. It would be better to be a king who stands strong, a simple household tool that serves its owner, or even a wooden door that protects a house than to be these lifeless idols. A wooden pillar in a palace is more useful than them.

The sun, moon, and stars shine brightly and obey God's command when sent on a mission. Lightning flashes across the sky for all to see, and the wind blows everywhere. When God orders the clouds to cover the earth, they follow his command. Fire burns mountains and forests when sent from above. But these idols have no power or purpose and should not even be compared to these forces of nature.

That is why no one should think of them as gods or call them gods. They cannot decide what is right or wrong, and they do nothing to help anyone. Since you now understand that they are not gods, do not fear them.

They cannot bless or curse kings. They cannot make signs appear in the sky for the nations to see, shine like the sun, or give light like the moon. Even wild animals are better than these statues because they can at least run for shelter and protect themselves. There is no proof that these idols are gods—so do not be afraid of them.

These false gods are as useless as a scarecrow in a cucumber field that protects nothing. They are like a thornbush where birds rest or like a lifeless body thrown into the dark. Their fine clothes of purple and linen will eventually rot away, proving they are not gods. In the end, they themselves will decay and become worthless.

It is far better to be an honest person who worships no idols—such a person will never be ashamed.

The Book of Baruch

Introduction to the Book of Baruch

The Book of Baruch is a special part of the Apocrypha, traditionally linked to Baruch, who was a scribe and close friend of the prophet Jeremiah. It focuses on important ideas like asking for forgiveness, seeking wisdom, and trusting in God's constant support. Many believe it was written during the time when the Israelites were exiled in Babylon, sharing their struggles and hopes while living far from home.

This book includes prayers, honest confessions, and words of encouragement. It emphasizes the importance of turning back to God with humility and following His teachings. It also reflects on wisdom, describing it as a gift from God and encouraging people to seek understanding by living according to His guidance.

Though the Book of Baruch is not part of the Hebrew Bible, many Christian traditions value it for its deep spiritual lessons and its powerful message of faith and renewal.

This book contains the writings of Baruch, the son of Nerias and grandson of Maasias, from the family line of Sedecias, Asadias, and Chelcias. He wrote these words while living in Babylon. It was the fifth year, on the seventh day of the month, after the Chaldeans had taken over Jerusalem and burned the city down.

Baruch read these words aloud to Jechonias, the son of Joachim and king of Judah, as well as to everyone who had gathered to listen. He also shared them with the nobles, the king's sons, the elders, and all the people, from the poorest to the most powerful, who lived near the river Sud in Babylon.

Chapter 1

These are the words written by Baruch, the son of Nerias and grandson of Maasias, who came from the family of Sedecias, Asadias, and Chelcias while he was living in Babylon.

It was the fifth year, on the seventh day of the month, after the Chaldeans had taken over Jerusalem and burned it down. Baruch read these words aloud to Jechonias, the son of Joachim and king of Judah, as well as to everyone who had gathered to listen. He also read them before the nobles, the king's sons, the elders, and all the people, from the poorest to the most powerful, who lived near the river Sud in Babylon.

When they heard these words, the people wept, fasted, and prayed to God. They also collected money, each giving whatever they could. This offering was sent to Jerusalem to Joachim, the high priest, who was the son of Chelcias and grandson of Salom, along with the other priests and people living there.

At that time, Joachim received the holy objects that had been taken from the Lord's temple. These sacred items were returned to Judah on the tenth day of the month of Sivan. Among them were silver vessels made by Sedecias, the son of Josias, king of Judah.

This happened after Nebuchadnezzar, the king of Babylon, had taken Jechonias, along with the nobles, soldiers, and many people from Jerusalem, and brought them to Babylon.

They sent a message saying: "We are sending you money to buy offerings, including burnt offerings, sin offerings, and incense. Use it to prepare the grain offerings and present them on the altar of the Lord our God.

Also, pray for the lives of Nebuchadnezzar, king of Babylon, and his son Balthasar, that they may live long lives. May the Lord give us strength and wisdom so that we can live safely under their rule. We will serve them for a long time and hope to be treated well by them.

Pray to the Lord our God for us, too, because we have sinned against Him. Even now, His anger has not turned away from us.

Read this book we are sending to you and confess your sins in the Lord's house during the holy feasts and special days of worship.

Say these words: 'The Lord our God is righteous, but we are full of shame, as we see today—this is true for the people of Judah and Jerusalem, as well as for our kings, princes, priests, prophets, and ancestors.

We have sinned against the Lord. We disobeyed Him and ignored His commands.

From the time He rescued our ancestors from Egypt until today, we have continued to turn away from Him and refused to listen. That is why we are suffering now. The curse that God warned us about through His servant Moses has come upon us. He spoke these words when He brought our ancestors out of Egypt to give them a land filled with good things, just as it is today.

But even then, we refused to listen to God's voice or follow the messages of the prophets He sent. Instead, we followed our own stubborn and sinful ways, worshiping false gods and doing evil in the eyes of the Lord our God.'"

Chapter 2

The Lord has done exactly what He warned us about—bringing judgment on our judges, kings, leaders, and all the people of Israel and

Judah. He allowed terrible disasters to happen to us, worse than anything seen before, just as it was written in the Law of Moses. Things became so desperate that people were forced to eat their own children.

He handed us over to our enemies, making us a laughingstock among the nations where we were scattered. Instead of being honored, we were humiliated because we sinned against the Lord and refused to listen to Him.

The Lord is just, but we and our ancestors are covered in shame, as we can clearly see even now. Even after all these troubles, we still haven't turned back to Him or changed our wicked ways. Because of this, He made sure that disaster came upon us, just as He said He would. He is always right in what He commands, yet we still have not obeyed Him or followed the way He told us to live.

Now, Lord God of Israel, You rescued Your people from Egypt with great power, performing miracles that are still remembered today. But we have sinned, done wrong, and disobeyed You.

Please turn Your anger away from us. We are few in number compared to the nations where You scattered us. Hear our prayers, Lord, and save us for the sake of Your name. Let those who rule over us show us kindness and mercy.

Let the world know that You are our God, for we, the people of Israel, bear Your name. Look down from Your holy place, Lord, and see our suffering. Listen to our cries and notice our pain. The dead, who have already passed away, can no longer praise or worship You.

But those who are still alive, those who are weak and struggling, with weary hearts and hungry bodies, will praise You and seek righteousness, Lord. We do not come before You because of the goodness of our ancestors or kings, but because Your anger has been poured out on us, just as You warned through Your prophets.

You told us: "If you serve the king of Babylon, you will remain in the land I gave to your ancestors. But if you refuse to listen and do not serve him, I will take away all joy from Judah and Jerusalem—there will be no more weddings, no more celebrations. The land will become empty and abandoned."

But we didn't listen. We refused to serve the king of Babylon, and so You carried out what Your prophets warned about. The bones of our kings and ancestors were taken from their graves and left exposed to the sun by day and the cold by night. Many people died in misery—by hunger, war, and disease.

Your temple, the house that carries Your name, was destroyed because of the sins of Israel and Judah. Yet despite all of this, Lord, You have treated us with kindness and mercy, just as You promised through Moses when You gave him Your laws for Israel.

You said: "If you do not obey Me, this great nation will become small and scattered among foreign lands. I knew you would not listen because you are stubborn. But in exile, you will come to your senses. You will realize that I am the Lord your God because I will give you understanding and open your ears to hear.

In their captivity, My people will remember Me and praise My name. They will repent, turning away from their stubbornness and sins, realizing how their ancestors also rebelled against Me. Then I will bring them back to the land I promised to Abraham, Isaac, and Jacob. They will take possession of it, and I will bless them so they will never be few in number again.

I will make a lasting promise to them: I will be their God, and they will be My people. Never again will I take Israel out of the land I have given them."

Chapter 3

O Lord Almighty, God of Israel, those who are suffering and burdened with sorrow cry out to You. Please hear us, Lord, and show us Your mercy, for You are full of kindness. Have compassion on us, for we have sinned against You. You remain eternal, but we are fading away.

O Lord Almighty, God of Israel, listen to the prayers of those who have passed away and to their children, who have sinned and refused to obey You. Because of this, we are suffering under these troubles. Please do not hold the sins of our ancestors against us. Instead, remember Your great power and Your name at this moment. You are our God, and we will praise You, Lord.

You have placed reverence for You in our hearts so that we would call on Your name and honor You, even while living in captivity. We have reflected on the sins of our ancestors who disobeyed You. Even now, we remain scattered, facing shame and hardship. We are burdened under the rule of others because of the sins of those who turned away from You, our God.

Listen, Israel, to the commandments that bring life. Pay attention so that you may gain wisdom. How did this happen to you, Israel? You now live in a foreign land, growing old far from home, surrounded by death and counted among those who have no future. You have turned away from the source of wisdom.

If you had followed God's ways, you would have lived in peace forever. Seek wisdom, find where strength and understanding begin, so that you may discover the path to a long life, clear vision, and true peace. Who has entered her dwelling place? Who has found her hidden treasures?

Where are the leaders of the nations, the ones who ruled over wild beasts? Where are those who played among the birds and gathered silver and gold, trusting in their riches and collecting endless treasures? Where are the craftsmen who worked skillfully with silver, creating masterpieces? They have all disappeared into the grave, and others have taken their place.

People are born, see the light of day, and live on the earth, but they have not found the way to knowledge. They do not understand wisdom's path or embrace her. Their descendants remain far from her ways. Wisdom has not been found in Canaan or in the land of Teman.

The descendants of Hagar, those who search for earthly wisdom, the traders of Meran and Teman, the storytellers, and those who seek understanding—none of them have discovered the path of wisdom or remembered her ways.

O Israel, how great is God's dwelling place, and how vast is His land! It stretches beyond what anyone can measure. Even the tallest giants of ancient times, men known for their great size and skill in battle, were not chosen by the Lord. He did not reveal wisdom to them. They perished because they lacked understanding and acted foolishly.

Who has gone up to heaven to take hold of wisdom and bring her down from the clouds? Who has crossed the seas to find her and bring her back, like a precious treasure? No one knows the way to her or understands her path.

But the One who knows everything understands wisdom. He alone found her. He is the One who created the earth to last forever and filled it with every living creature. He commands the light, and it appears; He calls it back, and it obeys Him with respect. The stars take their places and shine with joy. When He calls them, they answer, "Here we are," and they shine gladly for the One who created them.

This is our God, and there is no one like Him. He has discovered all the ways of wisdom and shared them with Jacob, His servant, and Israel, His chosen people. Later, He appeared on earth and lived among us.

Chapter 4

This is the book of God's commandments and His everlasting law. Those who follow it will find life, but those who turn away from it will face destruction. Return to it, Jacob, and hold on to it tightly. Walk in its light so that you may grow in understanding.

Do not give away your honor or let foreign nations take what was meant for your good. Israel, you are truly blessed because God has shown you what pleases Him. Stay strong, my people, who carry the memory of Israel.

You were not given to the nations to be destroyed, but because you angered God, He allowed you to fall into the hands of your enemies. You turned against the One who created you by worshiping false gods instead of Him. You forgot the eternal God who raised you up, and because of that, Jerusalem, the city that cared for you, was filled with sorrow.

When Jerusalem saw God's anger fall upon you, she said, "Listen, everyone who lives near Zion. The Lord has brought great sorrow upon me. I have watched my sons and daughters taken away as captives by the Eternal One. I raised them with joy, but now I send them away with tears and grief.

Do not celebrate over me, a widow left abandoned, made empty because of the sins of my children. They turned away from God's law and did not follow His commands. They ignored His teachings and failed to live in righteousness.

Let everyone near Zion remember how my sons and daughters were taken captive by the Eternal One. He sent against them a distant nation, a people without shame, speaking a foreign language. They had no respect for the elderly and no pity for children. They took away my beloved children and left me alone without daughters.

But what can I do for you? The One who allowed this suffering will also rescue you from your enemies. Go your way, my children, for I am left alone. I have taken off my clothes of peace and put on sackcloth to pray. I will cry out to the Eternal One for the rest of my life.

Take heart, my children, and call on the Lord. He will save you from the power of your enemies. My hope is in the Eternal One, for I trust that He will rescue you. I rejoice in the mercy that will soon come to you from our everlasting Savior. Though I sent you away with sorrow, God will bring you back to me with unending joy and happiness.

Just as your neighbors in Zion saw you taken into captivity, they will soon see God's salvation come to you with great glory and the light of the Eternal One. My children, endure the suffering that God has allowed. Though your enemies have oppressed you, soon you will see them fall and walk over them in victory.

My dear ones have walked through hard times and been led away like sheep captured by their enemies. Stay strong, my children, and call on God. He will remember you and the struggles you have been through.

Just as you once turned away from God, now that you are coming back to Him, seek Him with even greater passion. The One who allowed this suffering will give you eternal joy and salvation. Take comfort, Jerusalem, for the One who gave you your name will bring you peace.

Those who made you suffer and rejoiced in your downfall will soon face hardship themselves. The cities that enslaved your children will be cursed. The nation that welcomed your captors will also be cursed. Just as they celebrated your suffering, they will soon mourn their own destruction.

I will take away their joy, and their pride will turn into sorrow. Fire from the Eternal One will consume them, burning for a long time, and their land will become empty, a place haunted for generations.

O Jerusalem, look to the east and see the joy coming to you from God. Look! Your children, whom you sent away, are returning home. They are being gathered from the east and the west by the word of the Holy One, rejoicing in the glory of God.

Chapter 5

Jerusalem, take off the clothes of sorrow and suffering, and put on the beauty of God's eternal glory. Wear the robe of righteousness that comes from Him, and place the crown of everlasting honor on your head, a gift from the Eternal One.

God will show the world your beauty, making it known to every nation under the sky. He will give you a name that will last forever: The Peace of Righteousness and The Glory of God's Worship.

Stand tall, Jerusalem, and hold your head high. Look to the east and see your children returning from the west, brought back by the word of the Holy One. They rejoice as they remember their God.

They were taken away on foot, led by their enemies, but now God is bringing them home with honor, lifted up as His children and heirs to His kingdom.

God has commanded that every high mountain and ancient obstacle be made low and every valley filled in, creating a smooth path so Israel can walk safely in His glory.

Even the forests and every fragrant tree will give shade to Israel, just as God has planned. The Lord will lead His people with joy, shining with the light of His glory, surrounded by His mercy and righteousness.

The Apocalypse of Baruch

Yerusalem will be destroyed.

Chapter 1~5

In the twenty-fifth year of King Jeconiah's reign over Judah, the Lord spoke to Baruch, the son of Neriah, and said:

"Do you see what these people are doing to me? The sins of the remaining tribes are even worse than those committed by the ten tribes who were taken into exile. The ten tribes were led astray by their kings, but these two tribes push their kings into sin.

Because of this, I will bring disaster upon this city and its people. They will be taken away from my presence for a time, and I will scatter them among the nations. Yet through them, other nations may be blessed. My people will go through discipline, but the time will come when they will seek the things that bring them peace and prosperity.

I am telling you this so you can warn Jeremiah and others like you to leave this city. Your actions are like a pillar that holds it up, and your prayers are like a strong wall protecting it."

And I said, "Lord, my God, did I come into this world only to witness the suffering of my people? No, my Lord. If I have found favor in your eyes, take my life first, so I may join my ancestors instead of seeing the destruction of my people.

I feel trapped, caught between two forces. I cannot go against You, yet my soul cannot bear to see my people suffer.

But I have one question, Lord. What will happen after all this? If You destroy this city and give our land to those who hate us, how will Israel ever be remembered?

Who will declare Your greatness? Who will teach others Your laws? Will the world return to chaos and silence? Will people's souls be taken away, and will the memory of humanity disappear forever?

And what about the promises You made to Moses about us?"

The Lord answered me, "This city will be taken for a time, and the people will face discipline, but the world will not be forgotten.

Do you think this city is the one I spoke about when I said, 'I have engraved you on the palms of my hands'? The city I was speaking of is not the one you see now. It is the one that will be revealed with me. It was prepared from the moment I created the Garden of Eden, and I showed it to Adam before he sinned.

When Adam disobeyed, this city and the Garden were taken from him. Later, I revealed it to Abraham during the night of the covenant, between the divided sacrifices.

I also showed it to Moses on Mount Sinai when I gave him the design for the tabernacle and all its furnishings.

Now, this city is kept safe with me, along with the Garden. Go now and do what I have commanded you."

I replied, "Then I will be guilty in Zion, for Your enemies will invade this land and desecrate Your holy place. They will take Your people as captives and rule over those You love.

They will return to their land filled with idols and brag about their victory. Lord, what will You do for Your great name?"

The Lord answered, "My name and my glory will last forever. My judgment will come at the right time.

You will see with your own eyes that the enemy will not destroy Zion or burn Jerusalem. Instead, they will serve the true Judge for a time.

But as for you, go and do all that I have commanded you."

So I gathered Jeremiah, Iddo, Seraiah, Jabesh, Gedaliah, and all the leaders of the people. I led them to the Kidron Valley and told them everything the Lord had spoken to me.

They lifted their voices and wept loudly. We sat together and fasted until evening.

Chapter 6~9

The next day, a Chaldean army surrounded Jerusalem. As evening fell, I, Baruch, stepped away from the people and left the city walls. I stood near an old oak tree, heartbroken over Zion and grieving for the people of Israel who were about to be taken into exile.

As I mourned, a powerful wind suddenly swept me off the ground. It carried me high above the walls of Jerusalem, giving me a full view of the entire city. As I looked down, I saw four angels standing at the four corners of the city, each holding a burning torch. Their flames glowed brightly, casting a strange and ominous light over Jerusalem.

Then, another angel descended from the sky, radiant and full of authority. He turned to the four angels holding the torches and said, "Hold your lamps steady and do not light them until I give the command. First, I must complete my task—delivering a message to the earth and carrying out the Lord's command."

I watched as the angel entered the Holy of Holies inside the temple. There, he gathered the most sacred objects: the veil, the holy ephod, the mercy seat, the two stone tablets of the law, the priests' holy garments, the altar of incense, the forty-eight precious stones from the priests' robes, and all the sacred vessels used in worship.

After collecting these items, the angel raised his voice and spoke to the earth:

"Earth, earth, earth, listen to the word of the Mighty God. I am entrusting you with these holy objects. Keep them safe until the appointed time. When the moment comes, you will return them so they will not fall into the hands of those who do not honor them.

For now, Jerusalem will be given over to destruction, but one day, it will be restored forever."

As soon as he finished speaking, the ground opened up and swallowed the sacred objects.

Then, the angel turned to the four holding the torches and commanded, "Now, bring down the walls of this city. Tear them to their very foundations so that our enemies cannot boast and say, 'We destroyed Zion and burned the house of the Mighty God.'"

After speaking, the angel returned me to my place near the oak tree.

Then, the angels carrying the torches began their work. They struck the four corners of the walls, and the entire structure collapsed. As the city crumbled, a voice echoed from within the temple, crying out:

"Enter now, enemies! Come forward, adversaries! The One who protected this house has now abandoned it."

With a heavy heart, I, Baruch, turned away and left.

Soon after, the Chaldean army stormed the city. They rushed into the temple, seizing everything inside and around it. They captured the people, taking many into exile, killing others, and leaving only a few survivors.

King Zedekiah was caught, bound, and taken as a prisoner to the king of Babylon.

I found Jeremiah, who was spared because of his pure heart and was not taken during the invasion. Together, we tore our clothes in sorrow and wept bitterly for Jerusalem. We mourned and fasted for seven days, grieving deeply for our people and our land.

Chapter 10~12

After seven days had passed, the word of God came to me, saying, "Tell Jeremiah to leave this place and go with the exiles to Babylon. He will encourage and support them there. But you, Baruch, must stay here in the ruins of Zion. In the coming days, I will show you what will happen at the end of time."

I did as the Lord commanded and told Jeremiah His words. Without hesitation, Jeremiah left with the people who were being taken into exile. Meanwhile, I, Baruch, returned to Jerusalem and sat in front of the gates of the Temple. Surrounded by the ruins of the holy city, I raised my voice and mourned for Zion:

"Blessed are those who were never born, or those who lived and have already passed away.

But as for us who remain, woe to us! We must witness Zion's suffering and the destruction of Jerusalem.

I call upon the sirens of the sea. Creatures of the wilderness, spirits of the desert, and monsters of the forests—awake! Come and mourn with me for the fall of Zion. Let us sing songs of sorrow together.

You, farmers, stop planting your fields. And you, earth, why do you still bring forth fruit? Hold back your harvest and keep it hidden.

You, vineyards, why do you still produce wine? No offerings will ever again be made from you in Zion, and the first fruits will never again be placed on the altar.

You, heavens, stop sending rain. Lock up the dew in your storehouses.

You, sun, stop shining. And you, moon, let your glow fade away. Why should light continue when Zion's radiance has been extinguished?

Bridegrooms, do not enter your wedding chambers. Brides, throw away your garlands.

Women, stop praying for children, for the barren will rejoice more than mothers. Those without children will find joy, but those with sons will only grieve.

Why should mothers endure the pain of childbirth, only to bury their children in sorrow? Why should fathers bring sons into a world where they will be taken into exile or killed?

From now on, do not speak of beauty or gracefulness, for they are no longer found in this land of ruin.

Priests, take the keys to the Temple and throw them toward the heavens. Say to the Lord, 'Guard Your house Yourself, for we were unworthy caretakers and have failed You.'

And you, young women who weave fine garments with gold from Ophir, gather your treasures and throw them into the fire. Let the flames carry them back to the One who created them, so our enemies do not take them for themselves."

Then I turned my sorrow toward Babylon and said,

"Babylon, if Zion had remained glorious while you prospered, it would have been unbearable to see you as her equal. But now, our grief is endless, and our sorrow has no measure. Zion is in ruins, while you thrive.

Who will judge these injustices? To whom can we cry out for fairness?

O Lord, how can You bear this? Our ancestors died without witnessing this suffering. The righteous rest in peace underground, unaware of the pain we now endure.

If only the earth had ears to hear and a heart to understand! If only the dust could send a message to the dead, telling them, 'You are more fortunate than those who are still alive.'

But I will speak the thoughts of my heart. I will cry out against you, O land of prosperity:

The sun does not shine endlessly at noon, and its light does not last forever. Do not think your wealth and power will never end. Do not be arrogant or oppress others, thinking you will always remain above them.

For judgment will rise against you at the appointed time. Though the Lord's patience holds it back for now, it will surely come."

After speaking these words, I fasted for seven days, filled with sorrow and prayer.

Chapter 13~15

After all these things happened, I, Baruch, stood on Mount Zion, looking at the ruins of the city, lost in thought. Suddenly, a voice from above called out to me:

"Stand up, Baruch, and listen to the words of the Mighty God. You are shocked by what has happened to Zion, but know this: you will be kept safe until the end of time so that you can be a witness.

When the great cities of the world ask, 'Why has God allowed such destruction?' you and others who have seen this disaster will be able to answer them, saying, 'This happened so that all nations could be judged for their actions.'

And if they ask, 'When will this judgment come?' you must say:

'You who enjoyed the sweet wine of success, now drink the bitter cup of suffering, for God's judgment is fair.

He did not even spare His own people when they sinned but punished them like enemies so they might be forgiven. But you, the nations of the world, have also done wrong. You have mistreated the earth and used its gifts selfishly.

You have taken all the good things God created, yet you have shown no gratitude for His blessings.'"

Hearing this, I said, "You have shown me the future and how judgment will come upon the nations.

But I do not understand. Many who have done evil have lived comfortable lives and died peacefully. When the time of judgment comes, few will be left to hear Your words.

What is the point of knowing this, Lord? What punishment could be worse than what we have already suffered?

Yet I will continue to ask You: What good is it for those who have lived righteously, those who have stayed away from the ways of the world and never sought answers from the dead?

These faithful ones have feared You and followed Your ways. And yet, You allowed Zion to be destroyed without mercy, even though these good people lived there.

If others have sinned, should Zion not have been spared for the sake of the righteous? Why was she destroyed because of the wicked?"

I paused, then asked, "Who, O Lord, can understand Your judgment? Who can comprehend Your ways or grasp the greatness of Your plan?

No one born on earth can fully understand the depth of Your wisdom.

We are as brief as a passing breath. Just as a breath disappears, so does human life. We do not leave this world by our own choice, and we do not know what will happen to us after we are gone.

But the righteous have hope in the end. They leave this life without fear, trusting in the good deeds they have stored with You. These are treasures kept safe in Your heavenly storehouses.

So they depart with peace and confidence, knowing that a better world awaits them.

But woe to us who remain, suffering and waiting for even more hardship. You, Lord, know everything about Your creation and why You made us. We cannot understand goodness as You, our Creator, do.

Still, I will speak. In the beginning, before the world existed, You spoke a single word, and creation came to life.

You made humanity to rule over the earth so that it would be clear that the world was created for them, not the other way around.

Yet now, I see that the world continues, but we, the ones it was made for, pass away."

Then the Lord answered me, "You are right to be amazed at how short man's life is. But your understanding of why the wicked prosper and the righteous suffer is incomplete.

You have said that people cannot understand My judgment, and that is true. But listen carefully, and I will explain it to you.

If I had not given humanity My law and taught them wisdom, they would not be able to understand My justice. But now that they have received knowledge and still choose to do wrong, they will be judged according to what they know.

As for the righteous, for whom you say the world was created: their true reward is not in this world, but in the world to come.

This life is full of hardship and struggle for them, but the next life will be their crown of glory—a reward far greater than anything this world could offer."

Chapter 16~20

I replied, "O Lord, my God, our lives are short and full of struggles. How can anyone, in such a brief and difficult life, inherit something infinite and beyond measure?"

The Lord answered me, "With the Most High, time is not measured by how long or short it is. Think about Adam—he lived for 930 years, but what good did all those years do him? His disobedience brought death upon himself and shortened the lives of all his descendants.

But look at Moses—he lived only 120 years. Yet, because he obeyed the One who created him, he was able to bring the law to the descendants of Jacob. Through his faithfulness, he became a guiding light for the people of Israel."

I then said, "The one who lit the lamp shared its light, but so few have followed it. Instead of rejoicing in the light he gave, many have chosen the darkness of Adam and refused the guidance of the lamp."

The Lord replied, "That is why I made a covenant with them long ago and declared, 'I have set before you life and death.' I called the heavens and the earth as witnesses against them. I knew their time would be short, but the heavens and the earth will endure forever.

Even after death entered the world, they continued to sin, despite having the law to guide them. They were given the light of truth without fault, yet they chose rebellion. They had witnesses—the heavens, the earth, and even Me—yet they still turned away.

Now, everything that exists is under My judgment.

But you, Baruch, do not dwell on the past or let it trouble your heart. Instead, focus on the end of time, for the conclusion is what truly matters.

Think about this: If a man enjoys prosperity in his youth but suffers disgrace in his old age, he forgets the good times. But if a man struggles when he is young but finds success in his later years, he no longer remembers his past hardships.

In the same way, even if every person had lived in endless prosperity since the day death entered the world, it would all be meaningless if destruction was waiting for them in the end."

Then the Lord continued, "Look, the days are coming when time will move faster than ever before. The seasons will pass more quickly than those that have come before, and the years will fly by even faster than they do now.

That is why I have taken Zion away—so that I may soon bring about the appointed time when I will visit the world in judgment.

Now, Baruch, hold tightly to everything I have commanded you. Keep My words deep in your heart and never forget them.

Prepare yourself, for soon I will reveal My great judgment and My mysterious ways to you.

So, set yourself apart for seven days. During this time, do not eat bread, do not drink water, and do not speak to anyone.

After these seven days, return to this place, and I will appear to you. I will reveal truths to you and show you what is to come. These things will not be delayed—they will happen just as I have planned."

Chapter 21

Then I left and went to the Kidron Valley, where I found a cave and sat inside. There, I dedicated myself to the Lord, setting my heart apart for Him. During those days, I ate no bread, yet I did not feel hungry. I drank no water, yet I did not feel thirsty. I remained in the cave for the full seven days, just as He had commanded me.

After the seven days, I got up and returned to the place where He had spoken to me before. It was sunset, and as the sky darkened, my mind became filled with deep thoughts. In that quiet moment, I began to speak before the Mighty One:

"O Lord, Creator of the earth, hear me! You, who spoke the heavens into place and set them high above by Your power. At the beginning of time, You called into existence what did not yet exist, and it obeyed Your command.

You are the one who controls the movement of the air and the forces of nature with a simple sign. You see everything—what has already happened and what is still to come. With Your great wisdom, You rule over the countless holy ones who stand before You, glowing like flames of fire, whom You created to surround Your throne.

Everything that exists belongs to You alone, and at any moment, You have the power to bring forth whatever You desire.

You count every drop of rain before it falls to the earth. You know the end of time before it even begins. Please hear my prayer, for You alone sustain all things—those who live now, those who have passed, and those yet to come.

You, O Lord, are the Living One, the Unchanging One, the Eternal One. You alone know the number of mankind. Though many throughout history have sinned, many others have walked in righteousness.

You understand the destiny of both the wicked and the righteous. You have set the final outcome of each one.

If this life is the only one we have, then nothing could be more painful than knowing how temporary it is. What good is strength if it fades into weakness? What is the purpose of plenty if it turns into hunger? What is the value of beauty if it is taken away by time and decay?

Human life is always changing. What we were before, we are no longer; and what we are now, we will not always be. If nothing had an end, then its beginning would have had no purpose.

Lord, show me Your wisdom. Help me understand what I ask of You: How long will corruption continue? How much longer will human life go on as it is?

When will those who die be free from the wickedness of this world?

In Your mercy, bring to pass all that You have promised, so that those who think Your patience is weakness may see Your power.

Let those who do not understand—who see what has happened to us and to our city—realize that all these events fit within Your plan. You have called us Your people for the sake of Your great name.

But now, everything is ruled by death. I beg You, Lord, hold back the power of death. Let Your glory shine through. Let the beauty of Your presence be revealed for all to see.

Close the gates of the grave so that it no longer takes in the dead.

Let the souls that have been waiting be released from their resting place. Many years have passed since the days of Abraham, Isaac, and Jacob—those who sleep in the earth, for whose sake You said You created the world.

Now, Lord, let Your glory be revealed without delay. Fulfill Your promises. Do not wait any longer."

When I finished praying, all my strength left me, and I felt completely weak.

Chapter 22~30

Then, the heavens opened before me, and I saw an incredible sight. A surge of strength filled me, reviving my spirit. I stood in awe as a voice from above spoke to me:

"Baruch, Baruch, why are you so troubled? Why is your heart weighed down with concern?

Who starts a journey and does not try to reach the end? Who sails out to sea without hoping to reach the shore safely?

Who promises to give a gift but never follows through? Wouldn't that be the same as stealing?

Who plants seeds in the ground but never expects to harvest them when the time is right? Or who plants a young tree and expects it to bear fruit before it has fully grown?

Doesn't a mother risk her child's life if she gives birth too soon? And isn't a house unfinished if it is built without a roof?

Tell me, are these things not true?"

I replied, "Yes, Lord, they are true."

Then He said, "If you understand this, then why are you troubled by things that are not yet clear to you? Why does your heart worry over matters you cannot yet understand?

Do you not realize that just as you remember those who live now and those who have passed, I also remember those who are yet to come?

When Adam sinned and death was passed on to all his descendants, I already knew how many souls would be born into this world. For each one, I prepared a place for the living and a place for the dead.

No soul will live again until the number I have set is complete. My Spirit is the source of all life, and the realm of the dead exists to receive those who have passed away.

But I have chosen to reveal to you what lies ahead. The time of redemption is closer now than ever before.

The days are coming when the books will be opened. These books hold the record of every sin committed by those who have turned away from Me. At the same time, the storehouses will be opened, revealing the righteousness of all who have walked in faith and obedience since the beginning of time.

In that day, you and many others will see with your own eyes the endless patience and mercy of the Most High. My patience has lasted through every generation, extending to both the righteous and the sinners.

The time is near when everything will be revealed and brought to completion."

I replied, "But Lord, no one knows how many things have already passed away, nor how many are still to come. I understand what has happened to us, but I do not know what will happen to our enemies or when You will bring justice."

The Lord answered, "You will be kept safe until the appointed time. When the sign that I have determined appears on the earth, it will mark the beginning of the final days.

This sign will bring fear and suffering upon the world. People will experience such deep trouble and pain that they will say in their hearts, 'The Mighty One has abandoned the earth.' But when they lose all hope, that is when the time of awakening will begin."

I asked, "Lord, how long will this time of suffering last? Will it continue for many years?"

The Lord replied, "This time has been divided into twelve distinct parts, each with its own purpose:

1. In the first part, there will be chaos and unrest.
2. In the second, the powerful will be overthrown.
3. In the third, many will die."

In the fourth part, violence and war will spread among the people.
In the fifth part, there will be famine, and the rain will stop.
In the sixth part, great disasters and earthquakes will shake the earth.

In the seventh part, spirits will roam, and demons will attack.

In the eighth part, fire will fall from the sky.

In the ninth part, there will be widespread oppression and terrible crimes.

In the tenth part, injustice and immorality will increase everywhere.

In the eleventh part, chaos will rise as all these troubles mix together.

And in the twelfth part, everything will reach its peak, as all these disasters become one.

"These times will be connected, each event affecting the others. Some will hold back their full force, while others will grow stronger. Those who live during this time will not realize they are witnessing the end of days. But those who have wisdom will understand, for this time has been measured as two periods of seven weeks."

I answered, "It may be a blessing to live and witness these events, but it could also be dangerous, for the risk of failure will be great. But Lord, let me ask—will these disasters only happen in one place, or will the whole earth experience them?"

The Lord replied, "These events will affect the entire world, and all people will experience them. But during this time, I will protect those who live in this land. When everything has been fulfilled, the Anointed One will begin to be revealed.

At that time, Behemoth will come out of its hidden place, and Leviathan will rise from the depths of the sea. These two great creatures, which I created on the fifth day of creation, have been kept for this very moment. They will provide food for those who survive. The earth will produce an abundance of crops, yielding a harvest ten thousand times greater than before.

Each vine will grow a thousand branches, each branch will have a thousand clusters, each cluster will hold a thousand grapes, and each grape will produce a large measure of wine. Those who once suffered from hunger will rejoice, for they will see miracles every day.

Each morning, a sweet breeze will come from My presence, carrying the scent of the fruits of paradise. In the evening, the clouds will release a dew that brings healing to all. And during those days, the storehouse of manna will open again from heaven, providing food for My people. These will be the ones who have reached the end of time.

After these events, when the Anointed One's time is fulfilled, He will return in glory. All those who have died, hoping for His coming, will rise again. The places where the souls of the righteous have been kept will be opened, and they will come forth together as one united people.

The first will rejoice, and the last will have no reason to be sad, for they will all see that the promised end has come.

But the souls of the wicked will see these things and be filled with fear. They will realize that their time of suffering has arrived, and their destruction is near."

Chapter 31~34

After these events, I gathered the people and said, "Bring together all the elders of Israel, for I have something important to tell you." They listened, and soon the elders and the people assembled in the Kidron Valley. Standing before them, I spoke with urgency:

"Listen to me, O Israel, and hear my words. Pay close attention, descendants of Jacob, for I will share wisdom with you. Do not forget

Zion, and do not let the suffering of Jerusalem fade from your hearts. Remember her pain and mourn for her.

The time is coming when everything you see now will fade away. It will be as if it never existed, disappearing into nothingness.

But as for you, if you prepare your hearts and hold tightly to the law, it will protect you when the Mighty One shakes the world. A time of great trouble is near, and it will test everyone. After this short period, Zion will be shaken so that it can be rebuilt. However, know this—the new city will not last forever. It will once again be torn down and left in ruins for a time.

But do not lose hope, for after that, Zion will be restored in glory, and its beauty will last forever.

Do not let the hardships you face now break your spirit. Instead, prepare yourselves for what is coming, for the challenges ahead will be even greater than those you have already endured. When the Mighty One renews His creation, the struggles of humanity will be more difficult than anything before.

Therefore, stay strong and keep watch.

For now, I ask you for this one thing: do not look for me for the next few days. I need time alone, for I must speak with the Mighty One. When I return, I will share with you what He reveals to me."

After saying these words, I turned and began to walk away. As the people watched me leave, they cried out loudly in sorrow:

"Where are you going, Baruch? Are you leaving us now, like a father abandoning his children? Will you leave us as orphans in our time of need?

Didn't your companion, Jeremiah the prophet, entrust us to your care? Didn't he say, 'Look after the rest of our brothers while I go to Babylon to prepare those in exile'?

And now, if you leave us too, it would have been better for us to die than to see you go."

Hearing their cries, I turned back to them and said:

"I would never abandon you or turn away from you! My heart is with you, and I remain responsible for you. But I must go now—for your sake and for the sake of Zion—to the Holy of Holies. There, I will seek guidance from the Mighty One and ask for wisdom.

Do not fear, for when my task is done, I will return to you."

With that, I continued on my way, leaving their voices of sorrow behind me as I went to seek the presence of the Mighty One.

Chapter 35~43

I, Baruch, went to the holy place, sat among its ruins, and wept bitterly. I cried out, "Oh, if only my eyes were endless springs of water, and my tears never stopped flowing, so I could properly mourn for Zion and grieve for Jerusalem.

How can I find the right words to express my sorrow for this holy city? Here, where I now sit in ruins, the chief priests once stood, offering holy sacrifices to the Mighty One. The altar was covered with the most fragrant incense, and the air was filled with the sounds of worship.

But now, all our glory has turned to dust, and our deepest desires have been reduced to ashes beneath our feet."

After I spoke these words, overwhelmed by grief, I fell asleep among the ruins. As I slept, I had a vision in the night.

I saw a vast forest spread across a wide plain, surrounded by tall mountains and jagged rocks. The forest stretched far and wide, covering much of the land. As I watched, a vine appeared before the forest, and from beneath the vine, a peaceful fountain began to flow. The water from the fountain grew stronger as it reached the forest, turning into mighty waves.

The waves crashed into the trees, uprooting them and knocking down the mountains that surrounded them.

The forest was brought low, and the once-great mountains were leveled. The waves grew stronger and stronger until only one tree remained—a single cedar. When the waves finally reached this last tree, they knocked it down with such force that the entire forest was completely destroyed. Nothing remained of its former greatness, and no one could even recognize where it once stood.

Then, the fountain and the vine moved peacefully together to a place near where the cedar had fallen. Strangely, the cedar was brought before the fountain and the vine, as if it were about to be judged.

As I watched, the vine opened its mouth and spoke to the cedar:

"Are you not the last of the cedars from this wicked forest? You allowed evil to thrive for years, and because of you, unrighteousness continued to spread.

You did nothing good. Instead, you reached into lands that were not your own, showing no kindness even to what belonged to you. You trapped those far from you in your web of wickedness, and those near you were crushed under your power.

You believed you could never be moved, but now your time has come, and your judgment is here.

So now, cedar, join the rest of the forest that has already fallen before you. Turn to dust, and let your ashes mix with theirs. Rest in suffering and sorrow, for your final punishment has not yet come. When the appointed time arrives, you will return to face an even greater judgment."

After these words, I saw the cedar catch fire and burn until it was completely consumed. Meanwhile, the vine grew stronger, spreading across the land. The ground around the vine became a beautiful plain, filled with flowers that never faded. The place radiated beauty and peace.

Then I awoke and rose from where I had been sleeping.

Shaken by the vision, I prayed earnestly to the Mighty One:

"O Lord, my God, You guide those who seek understanding. You have made Your law the source of life, and Your wisdom leads us on the right path.

Please help me understand this vision. Show me its meaning, for You know that my soul has always followed Your law and that I have never turned away from Your wisdom since my earliest days."

The Lord answered me:

"Baruch, I will explain the vision you have seen. The great forest surrounded by rugged mountains represents the kingdoms that have ruled over the earth. These are the kingdoms that have risen against Zion.

Listen, for the days are coming when the first kingdom that destroyed Zion will itself be destroyed. It will be conquered by another kingdom that will rise after it. This second kingdom will hold power for a time but will also fall. Then, a third kingdom will rise and rule, but it too will come to an end."

After this, a fourth kingdom will rise, stronger and more evil than the ones before it. It will rule over many people and spread its power far and wide, like a huge forest covering the land. This kingdom will see itself as the greatest, standing tall like the mighty cedar trees of Lebanon. But within it, truth will be hidden, and those who do wrong will find safety there, like wild animals hiding in a dense forest. Yet, when the right time comes, my Chosen One will appear, and he will tear down this kingdom and bring its power to an end.

The tall cedar tree that remained standing after the forest was destroyed represents this final kingdom. The words spoken to it by the vine show the judgment it will face. The vine and the fountain represent my Chosen One and the power of truth, which will bring peace and healing to the land. But the cedar tree and everything it stands for will be completely destroyed. This is the meaning of your vision, Baruch.

The last ruler of this kingdom will be captured and tied up, while his army will be wiped out by the sword. He will be brought to Mount Zion, where my Chosen One will confront him, revealing all his evil deeds and judging him for the actions of his armies. Nothing will be hidden—every crime will be exposed. Then, he will be put to death. My Chosen One will protect the rest of my people, those who have taken shelter in the place I have chosen for them. His rule will last forever, continuing until the world of corruption has come to its final end and everything I have planned has been completed. This, Baruch, is the vision you have seen and its true meaning.

Then I asked, "Lord, who will live to see these things happen? Who will be worthy of those times? Please allow me to speak freely and share my thoughts. I see many of your people who have turned away from your ways, rejecting your law. But I also see others who have left behind their foolish ways and taken refuge under your protection, choosing to follow your will. What will happen to them, Lord? How will they be treated in the last days? Will they be judged fairly, each one receiving what they deserve?"

The Lord answered, "I will tell you the answer. The good things I have spoken of will come to those who have believed in me, but those who have rejected me will receive the opposite. As for those who have come closer to me and those who have turned away, here is the meaning:

Those who once followed my law but later abandoned it, mixing with nations that do not know me, will be remembered for their former greatness before they fell, like tall mountains. But those who once lived without knowing the truth but later found it and joined my people will be honored for their transformation. Their later years will be like mountains, standing tall because of their change and dedication.

Time will pass from one period to another, and each season will follow the one before it, receiving from the past and continuing forward. In the end, everything will be judged at the right time. Those who belong to corruption will be taken by it, and those destined for life will receive it. The earth will be commanded to give back what it has taken, bringing forth all who have been buried when the moment comes."

Then the Lord said, "Baruch, keep your heart focused on everything I have told you. Understand and hold onto these words, for they bring comfort that will last forever. You will soon leave this world behind. You will forget everything that is temporary and never again think of the things of this life.

So now, go and tell your people to prepare for what is coming. Then return here and fast for seven days. After that, I will come to you again and reveal more to you."

Chapter 44~47

Then I, Baruch, left the place where I had received the message from God and returned to my people. I called for my oldest son, my trusted friend Gedaliah, and seven of the elders of the community. When they had all gathered, I spoke to them, saying:

"My time to leave this world has come, just as it does for everyone who lives on the earth. But you must remain strong and stay faithful to the law. Guard it carefully, and make sure the rest of the people do not turn away from the commandments of the Mighty One. Remember that the Creator we serve is fair and just in all his judgments.

Look at what has happened to Zion and consider what became of Jerusalem. These events prove that the Mighty One's judgment is right and that his wisdom is beyond our understanding. If you remain in awe of him, follow his laws, and do not turn away from his teachings, then the time of suffering will pass, and a time of comfort will come. Zion will be restored, and you will experience peace again.

The things of this world do not last. They are small and meaningless compared to what is coming. Everything that can decay will disappear, and everything that is mortal will come to an end. The pain and evil of this time will be forgotten, and no one will remember its sorrows. Those who chase after wealth and power now are wasting their efforts, for all their achievements will one day turn to nothing.

Do not place your hope in the present world, but in the one that is coming. That world will last forever. A new age is near, one where those who enter will never again be touched by corruption. In this new world, there will be no mercy for those who choose wickedness, and those who live there will never face destruction. It will be a world of purity and lasting peace.

This promised world is reserved for those who have sought wisdom, treasured understanding, and remained kind and faithful. They have held onto the truth and lived by it. This new world will belong to them, but those who reject it will face judgment.

So I urge you, warn the people with all your strength. This is your responsibility. If you guide and teach them, you will bring life to their souls."

When I finished speaking, my son and the elders were deeply saddened. They said to me, "Has the Mighty One truly humbled us so much that he will take you from us so soon? Will we be left in darkness, with no one to lead the people? Who will teach us the law? Who will help us know the difference between right and wrong?"

I replied, "I cannot go against the will of the Mighty One. But know this: Israel will always have a wise leader, and the tribe of Jacob will never be without a teacher of the law. You must prepare your hearts to follow the law and listen to those who have wisdom and understanding in the ways of the Lord. Stay strong and do not wander from the right path. If you do these things, the good promises I have spoken will come true for you, and you will not fall into the suffering I have warned you about."

I did not tell them the full truth about my departure, not even to my son, because the Mighty One had commanded me to keep it secret.

After I dismissed them, I told them, "I am going to Hebron because the Mighty One has sent me there." Then I left and arrived at the place where the Lord had spoken to me. There, I sat and fasted for seven days, waiting for what was to come.

Chapter 48~52

After seven days, I lifted my voice in prayer to the Mighty One and said:

"O Lord, you control the future, and time moves according to your will. You command the seasons to come and go, and they obey. The passing years follow the path you have set for them, and nothing can resist your eternal plan.

You alone know how long each generation will last, and you do not reveal all your secrets to everyone. You measure the size of the fire, control the winds, and see the highest heavens and the deepest darkness.

You keep track of those who will pass away and hold them according to your plan. You have prepared an eternal home for those yet to be born. You remember the very beginning of creation, when you brought everything into existence, and you have not forgotten the end, which has not yet come.

At your command, fire becomes obedient, changing into spirits that serve your will. By your word, you create life from nothing, and by your endless power, you sustain what is yet to come. With your wisdom, you guide all of creation, and you give understanding to the heavenly bodies so they can fulfill their purpose.

Countless angels stand ready before you, waiting for your command. They follow your instructions perfectly, carrying out their tasks in harmony and peace.

Now, listen to me, your servant, and hear my request. We, your creation, are here for only a short time, and just as quickly as we arrived, we return to dust. But to you, Lord, one hour is like an entire age, and one day is like a whole generation. Your understanding of time is beyond us.

Please do not be angry with us, for we are weak and temporary. Do not judge us too harshly, for what can we offer that is worthy of you? By your grace, we are brought into this world, yet we do not leave it by our own choice, but by your will.

We did not ask to be born, nor did we make plans for the afterlife. We have no power to stand under your judgment. What strength do we have that we could endure your wrath?

Show us compassion, Lord, and hold us up with your mercy. Only through your kindness and grace can we stand before you, the Creator of all things.

Look upon those who humble themselves before you, Lord, and rescue those who sincerely seek you. Do not take away the hope of your people, and do not end your mercy and salvation too soon. This is the nation you have chosen, the people you have set apart, unlike any other in the world.

Now I speak openly, sharing the thoughts in my heart. We have placed our trust in you, holding tightly to your law and cherishing its wisdom. Your commandments remain with us, and we know that as long as we follow them, we will not stumble.

We are blessed because we have stayed separate from the ways of other nations. We are united as one people, guided by the single law you have given us. This law belongs to us alone, and the wisdom you have placed in our hearts strengthens and sustains us."

When I finished praying, I felt weak, drained from pouring out my heart. Then the Mighty One answered me and said:

"Baruch, I have heard your prayer, and every word you have spoken has reached me. But understand this: my judgment follows its own course, and my law demands justice. I will answer you with the very words of your prayer and respond to your concerns.

Know this: nothing is ruined unless it first chooses to turn away from goodness, rejecting my patience and kindness. This is why I told you before that you would be taken up, and this promise still stands. The time of suffering will surely come. It will arrive suddenly, burning fiercely and sweeping through the world like a raging storm.

During those days, people will think they are living in peace, unaware that my judgment is near. The wise will become rare, and those who truly understand will be even harder to find. Many who once had knowledge will remain silent, withdrawing from the world.

Rumors will spread everywhere—some true, some false. Strange visions will appear, and many empty promises will be spoken—some completely baseless, others designed to deceive. Honor will turn into shame, and strength will crumble into disgrace. Confidence will break like fragile glass, and beauty will lose all value.

At that time, people will be confused and ask each other, 'Where has wisdom gone? Where can we find understanding?' And as these questions fill their minds, jealousy will grow among those who once felt small, and anger will consume those who were once peaceful. Wrath will stir up many, driving them to violence, and countless people will raise armies and spill blood. But in the end, they will all perish together, caught in the very destruction they sought to bring upon others."

These are the words spoken by the Mighty One—a warning for those willing to listen and a glimpse into what's coming.

"When that time arrives, it will be clear for all to see. The way things have always been will change. In the past, people sinned and hurt one another. Everyone chased after their own desires, thinking only of themselves and ignoring the laws of the Mighty One. They let their pride lead them away from the truth, choosing temporary pleasures instead of what lasts forever.

At that time, people's thoughts will be tested like metal in fire. The Judge will come in glory, and He will not be late. Deep down, everyone has known when they were doing wrong, but their pride kept them from admitting it. Because they ignored my law, they will mourn—not just for themselves, but for those still alive, because they will finally understand the weight of their mistakes and the price they must pay.

Then I, Baruch, spoke, saying, 'Oh Adam, what have you done to all your children? And Eve, what trouble has come from listening to the serpent? Because of you, so many have fallen into corruption, and countless souls will now face judgment.

But Lord, You know everything. You made Adam from the earth, and from him, all of humanity came to be. Only You know the number of people who have ever lived. You have seen how they turned against You, refusing to acknowledge You as their Creator. Because of this, they will face shame, and the law they ignored will stand against them when judgment comes.

But let's not speak of the wicked any longer—let's focus on the righteous. They have suffered much in this short life, but they will be rewarded with endless light in a world that never fades.

Now, Mighty One, tell me—what will happen to the living on that day? Will they keep these weak, mortal bodies, or will You change them along with the rest of creation?'

And He answered me:

'Baruch, listen carefully. Write down what I tell you because it is important. When the time comes, the earth will give back the dead. Right now, it holds them as they were when they died. And just as I placed them in the earth, they will return the same way. They will rise exactly as they were before.

This must happen so the living can see the truth—that the dead have come back, that those who were gone are now among them again. When people recognize their loved ones, they will know for certain that the resurrection is real, and this will make my judgment even more powerful. What has been promised will happen without a doubt.

After this, once that great day is over, both the wicked and the righteous will be changed. Those who lived in sin will suffer even more. Their appearance will become twisted, showing the pain and regret they feel. Their faces will be marked with fear and sorrow.

But the righteous—those who followed my law and sought wisdom—their beauty will shine. Their faces will glow with light, and they will be transformed in splendor. They will be ready to receive the everlasting world I have prepared for them. Their transformation will show their understanding and the wisdom they carried in their hearts.

Meanwhile, those who rejected my law and refused to listen to wisdom will be filled with sorrow. They ignored the truth, and now they will watch as those they once looked down on are lifted up in glory. The righteous will be raised to a place of honor, while the wicked will become unrecognizable, their suffering visible for all to see.

But the righteous will witness wonders beyond anything they ever imagined. They will see a world they never knew existed, a time and place hidden from them until now. Time will no longer have power over them. They will dwell in a new creation, as bright as the stars, as glorious as the heavenly messengers. Their beauty will change from one form to another, glowing brighter and brighter.

They will enter the Garden of Delight, and they will see the great living beings beneath my throne. They will behold the heavenly messengers who have been waiting for this moment.

Their glory will surpass even that of the messengers. The first ones will welcome the last, and the last will finally see those they had only heard about. Together, they will rejoice, for they have escaped the suffering of this world and are free from pain forever.

In this new world, they will never again feel sorrow. Their light will never fade, their joy will never end, and the hope they held onto will be fulfilled beyond their wildest dreams. Those who sought wisdom and truth will receive more than they ever expected. They will inherit the everlasting glory that was always meant for them.'

Then He said:

'Why, then, do people waste their lives chasing things that don't last? Why do they trade their souls for what has no true value? Long ago, they made their choice. They clung to a world that only brings suffering and grief, ignoring the promise of a place that will never decay. They turned their backs on the eternal glory I offered them, choosing a path that leads only to regret.'

And I responded:

'How can we forget those who are destined for suffering? Why do we mourn for those who have already died when a much greater sorrow is coming? Shouldn't we save our tears for the day of destruction ahead?

Still, I must ask—what will become of the righteous? How should they face these times? They should rejoice, for their suffering is only shaping them for what is to come. Why focus on the downfall of their enemies when they have a far greater reward ahead? They should prepare themselves for the blessings waiting for them. Their reward, stored up in the heavens, will be far greater than any of the hardships they endured in this world.'

After I had spoken, I became very tired, and I lay down and fell asleep in that place."

Chapter 53~54

I had a vision—an incredible and overwhelming sight that filled me with awe. I saw a massive cloud rising from the sea, unlike anything I had ever seen before. The cloud held swirling waters, both dark and light, mixing together in a chaotic motion. Within these waters, flashes of different colors appeared, blending in a way that was both beautiful and mysterious. At the very top of the cloud, powerful lightning shone brightly, cutting through the sky with an intense glow.

The cloud moved swiftly across the earth, as if driven by a purpose only it knew. Its shadow stretched far and wide, covering the land beneath it. Then, something strange happened—the cloud began pouring out its waters onto the earth. As I watched closely, I noticed that these waters were not the same.

First, the waters were dark, heavy, and full of gloom, spreading shadows wherever they fell. This lasted for a while, but then the waters changed. They became bright, filled with light and clarity, though they were not as strong as the dark waters. But after this brief moment of brightness, the darkness returned, heavier than before. This cycle continued twelve times—dark waters followed by bright, with the darkness always lasting longer and seeming more powerful.

At the end, the cloud released its final storm. This time, the dark waters were even blacker, and fire mixed within them. When these fiery waters hit the earth, destruction followed. Entire regions were consumed, the land trembled, and ruin spread everywhere.

But then, something incredible happened. The lightning that had been at the top of the cloud suddenly struck the earth with great force. It brought a light so brilliant that it illuminated the entire world. Under this glow, the places ruined by the dark waters began to heal. The destruction was undone, and life returned. But this lightning did more than just restore—it took control of the entire earth, bringing peace and shining with unstoppable brightness.

As I continued watching, I saw twelve rivers rise from the sea. These rivers moved toward the lightning, surrounding it and submitting to its power. Their waters were clear and pure, flowing in harmony with the light. A deep sense of awe and fear filled me, and I woke up from my vision, shaking.

I turned to the Mighty One, pouring out my heart before Him:

"Lord, You alone have known the secrets of the world since the beginning. Nothing is hidden from You. You see the deepest parts of the earth and the highest places in the heavens. You control time itself, setting each moment in its place.

Nothing is too hard for You, for all things obey Your word. With a single command, You hold together what is above and below. Your will shapes the course of history, and the ages move according to Your plan.

To those who honor You, You reveal what awaits them, giving them strength through Your wisdom. To those who do not know You, You break through their ignorance and open their eyes. You share

Your secrets with those who trust in You, those who follow Your path with faith."

"Now, Lord, since You have given me this vision, I ask that You also help me understand its meaning. You have opened my mind, and I know I have received answers to my questions. You have shown me how to praise You, how to lift up my voice in honor of Your name. Yet, I realize that no matter how much I try, I can never fully express Your greatness.

Even if every part of my body could speak and every strand of my hair became a voice, it still would not be enough to give You the praise You deserve. My words could never fully describe the wonder of Your works. My heart cannot truly grasp the depth of Your beauty, which goes beyond all human understanding.

Who am I, that You would choose to show me these things? Compared to so many others, I am nothing—yet You have shared these mysteries with me. I am humbled by Your kindness. Blessed is the woman who gave birth to me, for she brought into the world someone who has been allowed to hear Your word. I will not stay silent. I will proclaim Your greatness and speak of Your wonders without end.

For who else, O Mighty One, can do what You do? Who else can understand the depth of Your wisdom? Every thought You have brings life, and all creation moves by Your eternal plan. You have placed the fountains of light beside You, and beneath Your throne, You have stored up treasures of wisdom, waiting for those who seek You.

But those who reject Your truth will face destruction. Judgment is waiting for those who refuse to follow Your ways. Adam sinned, and death came upon the world, but each person is responsible for their own choices. Every human, descended from Adam, chooses their own future—some preparing for eternal glory, others walking toward their own downfall. Those who believe in You will receive the reward of their faith.

But those who persist in wickedness, those who live in rebellion against Your truth, will soon face disaster. Their refusal to see Your wisdom will bring their own downfall. They have ignored the beauty of Your creation, which is a constant reminder of Your power. Their mistake is not just Adam's sin—it is their own choice. Each person is like their own Adam, shaping their fate through their actions.

Yet, Lord, I ask You again—help me understand the meaning of what You have shown me. Open my mind to the answers I seek. In the end, You will hold the wicked accountable for their deeds, and You will honor the faithful according to their devotion.

You rule over Your people with wisdom and justice, guiding them with love. But those who refuse to turn from evil will be removed from among the righteous. Lord, help me understand Your ways, for Your judgments are always right, and Your reign lasts forever."

Chapter 55~68

After I finished my prayer, I looked for a quiet place to rest. I sat beneath the wide branches of a tree, hoping for a moment of peace. The shade gave me relief, but my thoughts remained heavy. As I sat there, I thought about how much goodness sinners had turned away from. They had rejected the kindness and mercy freely given to them, choosing instead a path that would lead to their destruction. I wondered how they could ignore the suffering that awaited them, even though they knew the consequences of their choices. They refused to listen to the warnings, acting as if nothing would happen to them.

While I was deep in thought, trying to understand why people would reject such mercy, I suddenly sensed the presence of someone near me. I looked up and saw an angel standing before me. It was Remiel, the angel in charge of true visions, sent to me with a message. His presence was both powerful and gentle, and when he spoke, his voice was clear and strong.

"Why are you so troubled, Baruch?" he asked. "Why do these thoughts fill your mind with worry? If just hearing about the coming judgment makes you feel this overwhelmed, how will you handle it when you actually see it happen? If thinking about the day of the Mighty One weighs you down, how will you endure when it arrives?

"If simply hearing about the suffering of the wicked upsets you, how much more will you be shaken when you witness it with your own eyes? If even the mention of what will happen on that day fills you with sorrow, imagine how much greater your reaction will be when the power of the Almighty is revealed—bringing justice to some and joy to others.

"But because you have sincerely sought understanding, the Most High has sent me to explain your vision. Listen carefully, for the Mighty One has shown you the course of time—both past and future—from the moment the world was created until its final fulfillment. He has revealed the times when falsehood ruled and the times when truth prevailed.

"The great cloud you saw rising from the sea and spreading over the earth represents the entire span of history, from the beginning until the end. When the Mighty One decided to create this world, it started as something small, designed with great wisdom. By His command, it came into existence, structured according to His plan and guided by His perfect knowledge.

"The first dark waters that poured from the cloud represent the sin of Adam, the first man. When Adam disobeyed, death entered the world before its time. Grief and suffering became part of life, and pain took root in the hearts of humanity. Work became difficult, hardship increased, and pride led many away from goodness. The underworld, once still, became a force that constantly demanded more, taking life after life.

"Because of Adam's fall, people began to have children, but this came with sorrow and struggle. Humanity, once noble and pure, was humbled. The goodness that once filled the earth faded away like a passing mist. What could be darker than this? What could be more painful? This, Baruch, is the meaning of the first dark waters you saw in your vision—it represents the suffering that began with Adam's sin and has continued ever since."

"But from this darkness, even greater darkness was born. The suffering of the world grew worse because people turned away from their true purpose. They not only brought harm upon themselves but even disturbed the order of heaven. In the beginning, the angels were free from sin, but some of them chose to leave their place. They came down to earth and had children with human women, breaking the law of the Almighty. Because of this, they were punished—chained and cast into torment, a reminder of what happens when one disobeys the Creator.

"However, the majority of the heavenly messengers remained faithful. They did not give in to temptation but stayed true to their purpose. Meanwhile, the people on earth who had abandoned righteousness were destroyed in the great flood. These events marked the time represented by the first dark waters in your vision."

After those dark times, you saw bright waters. These waters represent the time of Abraham, the father of faith, and his descendants—his son, grandson, and those who followed in their ways. During this time, even though the law had not yet been written, people still followed it in their hearts. They lived by the commandments and believed strongly in the coming judgment. This was when hope for a renewed world began to grow, and the promise of a future life was planted. These bright waters symbolize the faith and goodness that shone during those days.

Then came the third waters, dark once more. These waters represent the sins that spread among the nations after the passing of righteous men. Evil flourished, especially in Egypt, where people acted cruelly and enslaved the children of Israel. But even this time of darkness did not last forever. The wickedness was judged, and justice was done.

Next, you saw the fourth waters, bright and shining. These waters represent the time of Moses, Aaron, Miriam, Joshua, Caleb, and others who stood with them. During this time, the eternal law was given, shining like a lamp for those in darkness. It brought hope to the faithful and warned the wicked of judgment. The heavens shook as the Mighty One revealed great truths to Moses. He showed him the principles of the law, the future of the world, and the design of the holy place, which reflected the heavens.

God also revealed to Moses the depths of the abyss, the weight of the winds, and the number of raindrops. He showed him how divine anger could be held back and how patience could be abundant. Moses was given wisdom, knowledge, and understanding. He saw the greatness of the Garden, the final judgment, and the future world. He learned about offerings, the coming ages, and places of justice and hope. These bright waters symbolize a time of revelation and divine guidance.

Then came the fifth waters, dark and ominous. These represent the sins of the Amorites, their evil magic, and the corruption they spread. Even the children of Israel fell into sin during the time of the judges, despite seeing many signs from their Creator.

The sixth waters, bright and clear, show the time of David and Solomon. During this time, Zion was built, the holy place was dedicated, and many sinful nations were defeated. The people made countless offerings, and the land was filled with peace. Wisdom was shared in gatherings, and understanding flourished. The holy festivals were celebrated with joy, and rulers judged fairly. People followed the commandments truthfully, and the land was full of mercy. Zion became a powerful and glorious center. These bright waters reflect the harmony and goodness of that time.

The seventh waters, dark and heavy, represent the deep corruption caused by Jeroboam, who led Israel into idol worship by setting up two golden calves. Many kings after him continued in wickedness. Jezebel's influence spread evil, and the people of Israel worshiped false gods. Because of this, the land suffered—rain stopped, and famine became so severe that people even ate their own children. Eventually, nine and a half tribes were exiled as punishment for their sins. The king of Assyria, Shalmaneser, took them away and scattered them in foreign lands. Meanwhile, the surrounding nations continued in their own wickedness. These are the dark waters of the seventh vision.

The eighth waters, bright and full of light, represent the faithfulness of Hezekiah, king of Judah. During his time, the Assyrian king Sennacherib gathered a huge army to destroy Judah, capture Zion, and wipe out the remaining two and a half tribes. But Hezekiah trusted in the Mighty One, praying for help. He asked God to see how Sennacherib planned to destroy them and lift himself up in pride. Because Hezekiah was faithful, God heard his prayer and acted.

God sent his messenger, Remiel, who destroyed Sennacherib's massive army. Among them, 185,000 leaders—each with their own troops—were burned up by fire from within, yet their clothes and weapons remained untouched, showing the power of the Mighty One. Because of this miracle, Zion was saved, Jerusalem was rescued, and the people of Israel were freed from their troubles. They rejoiced, spreading the name of the Mighty One everywhere. These are the bright waters you saw.

The ninth waters, dark and filled with evil, represent the terrible sins of Manasseh, Hezekiah's son. He committed terrible crimes—killing good people, corrupting justice, shedding innocent blood, and dishonoring marriages. He destroyed the altars, stopped the sacred offerings, and removed the priests from the holy place. He even built an idol with five faces, as if to challenge God himself.

Because of his actions, God's anger was unleashed. Zion was torn down, and judgment fell on the remaining two and a half tribes, sending them into exile. Manasseh's sins were so great that God's glory left the holy place. Because of his wickedness, Manasseh was given the title "the impious one," and his fate was sealed in fire. Even though he prayed for forgiveness in the end, his life remained deeply flawed. His final judgment was symbolized when a bronze horse statue he had fallen into melted, showing his punishment. These are the ninth dark waters you saw.

The tenth waters, bright and pure, represent the faith and devotion of King Josiah of Judah. He fully committed himself to the Mighty One with all his heart and soul. He removed idols, purified the sacred objects, and restored the altar offerings. He honored the righteous and reinstated the priests. He got rid of magicians, sorcerers, and false prophets, burning them and their remains.

Josiah brought back holy festivals and the sabbaths, cleansing the land of wickedness. He made sure no one in his kingdom acted unjustly. Because of his faithfulness, he will receive an eternal reward and be honored by God in the last days. For his sake, and for those like him, the promised blessings were prepared. These are the bright waters you saw.

The eleventh waters, dark and sorrowful, represent the disaster that has fallen upon Zion. The city, once full of God's glory, has been destroyed. The heavens do not celebrate its fall, though the nations mock and rejoice, saying that Zion, which once ruled over others, has now been conquered.

Do you think the Mighty One is pleased by this? Does He take joy in seeing His city ruined? No, He does not. But His justice will be carried out in the end, for He is always fair.

Because of these events, those scattered among the nations will face great hardships. They will live in shame, and as long as Zion remains in ruins, the wicked nations will thrive. Where Zion's holy incense once rose, now there is only the smoke of sin. The land once ruled by Zion is now filled with corruption.

The king of Babylon, who destroyed Zion, will become proud and believe he has won against the people of the Mighty One. But his pride will not last forever. In the end, God will humble him, and he will fall. These are the dark waters of the eleventh vision.

The twelfth waters, bright and full of hope, represent a time of renewal. After many hardships, your people will face their greatest struggle yet—so great that it will seem like they are about to be wiped out. But they will be saved, and their enemies will fall before them. It will be a time of great celebration and victory.

After this, Zion will be rebuilt. Offerings will once again be placed on its altars, and priests will return to their sacred duties. The nations will come to honor Zion and recognize the power of its God, though their respect will not be as deep as before. But even after this restoration, many nations will fall, their power crushed by divine justice. These are the bright waters you saw, pointing to Zion's future redemption and renewal.

Chapter 69~76

The last waters you saw were darker and blacker than all the ones before them. These waters came after the twelfth and were gathered together. They represent the fate of the whole world, not just one nation or group of people, but all of humanity. From the very beginning, the Most High separated the times, because only He knows the future. His knowledge covers all of history and even what has not yet happened.

He saw the evil that people would do in the future and identified six different kinds of wickedness. In the same way, He also saw six types of righteousness—the good things that faithful people would do in His sight, as well as the acts of kindness and salvation that He Himself would bring at the end of time. These last waters are different from the others. They are not just black mixed with black or bright mixed with bright. Instead, they represent the final moments—the end of this age.

Now, listen to what these last black waters mean. They show the days that are coming soon, when this world reaches its end, and everything people have done—both good and bad—has come to completion. In those days, the Mighty One will shake everything. People's hearts will be full of fear, and confusion will spread everywhere, even among kings and leaders.

People will begin to hate one another, turning against even their closest friends and neighbors. They will stir up anger, creating conflicts and division. Those who were once looked down upon will rise to power, while the honorable will be brought low. The weak will gain control over the strong, the poor will rule over the rich, and the wicked will claim victory over the brave.

During this time, wisdom will be silenced, and foolish people will take over. People's dreams and ambitions will fail, and their efforts will lead nowhere. Even the strongest leaders will struggle to hold things together. Everything that once seemed stable will fall apart, and fear will take hold of everyone's hearts and minds.

When this happens, the world will be thrown into chaos and suffering. Many will die in wars, caught up in violence and destruction. Others will not survive the hardships of their time. Some will even be betrayed by their own family members and fellow countrymen. These are the final black waters, marking the end of this age, the last chapter before everything changes. It is the deep darkness before the new beginning that the Mighty One has planned for the righteous.

Then, the Most High will show a clear and powerful sign to the nations and people whom He has already chosen and prepared. These nations will rise up and fight against the rulers still in power. This battle will be massive, shaking the earth itself. But even those who survive the war will not be safe.

If someone escapes the battle, they will die in a great earthquake. If they survive the earthquake, they will be destroyed by fire. If they somehow make it through the fire, they will starve to death. There will be no place for the wicked to hide—no part of the world will be free from disaster.

In the end, those who survive—whether they won their battles or were completely defeated—will be gathered together and handed over to my Servant, the Anointed One. At that time, the whole world will turn against its own people, bringing judgment upon them. No one will escape what has been decided, for the Most High will restore justice and righteousness.

However, the holy land, chosen and set apart from the very beginning, will show mercy to its own people. It will protect them and keep them safe from the overwhelming destruction of those days. This is the vision you have seen, Baruch, and this is its meaning. I was sent to reveal these things to you because your prayer reached the Most High, and He has chosen to show you these hidden truths.

Now listen carefully about the bright lightning that comes after the final and darkest waters. This is the ultimate message: After all the signs I have told you about have happened—when confusion spreads across the nations, and the time of my Anointed One arrives—he will gather all the nations before him. Some will receive mercy and be saved, while others will face judgment and destruction.

Here is what will happen to the nations that are spared: Any nation that has not harmed Israel or mistreated the descendants of Jacob will be shown kindness. They will be allowed to continue, because even among these nations, some people will humbly submit to your people. But the nations that ruled over Israel or knowingly caused them harm will face judgment. They will not escape the consequences of what they have done.

After my Anointed One humbles and defeats all the powerful rulers of the earth, he will establish his throne and bring eternal peace. Joy will fill the world, and all of creation will finally find true rest. Healing will cover the earth like gentle rain, and sickness will disappear completely. There will be no more fear, sorrow, or suffering. The world will be wrapped in happiness like a warm cloak. No one will die too soon, and sudden disasters will be gone. Fighting, judgment, anger, envy, hatred, and all the things that bring pain and trouble will be removed forever. These are the things that have made life hard and bitter, but they will be no more.

Even the animals will live peacefully with people. Wild creatures will no longer be a danger, and they will live in harmony with humans. Snakes and dragons will come out of their hiding places and obey even a child. Women will no longer suffer pain in childbirth, and their children will be born easily, without struggle.

In those days, workers will no longer grow tired, and builders will not feel exhausted from their labor. The earth will produce food quickly and abundantly, and those who work the land will do so in peace. This is the time when everything that is temporary and corrupt will pass away, and something new and eternal will begin. It will be a world free from the evils of the past, full of goodness and lasting peace.

This, Baruch, is the meaning of the bright lightning that follows the final dark waters. It represents the completion of all things, the return of righteousness, and the beginning of a new world.

Then I responded and said:

"Who in all creation can compare to your endless goodness, O Lord? It is beyond human understanding.

Who can measure the depth of your mercy, which has no limits and lasts forever?

Who has the wisdom to grasp the fullness of your knowledge, which surpasses all human thought?

Who can describe the thoughts of your spirit, which move beyond what words can express?

Who among those born in this fleeting world can ever hope to reach such wisdom, unless you grant it through your mercy and compassion?

If your kindness did not extend to humanity—those you hold in your powerful right hand—we would have no strength to understand the mysteries of your ways. Only those you have chosen and written in your eternal book can be called to such knowledge.

But for those of us living now, if we recognize why we are here and submit ourselves to the One who led our ancestors out of Egypt with great power, we will reflect on the past and find joy in what has happened. We will look back with gratitude, seeing the purpose behind it all.

However, if we ignore the reason for our existence and refuse to acknowledge the One who freed us from slavery in Egypt, we will struggle to understand the meaning of the present. And when the truth finally becomes clear to us, we will be filled with sorrow, realizing too late that we missed the chance to live according to your purpose."

Then the Most High answered me and said:

"Now that I have shown you this vision and its meaning, listen carefully so you can understand what will happen to you after these events.

You will leave this world, but not through death. Instead, you will be set apart and kept safe until the end of time, when everything I have planned is fulfilled.

Now, go up to the top of the mountain, and I will show you the land stretched out before you. You will see not only the size of this world but also the image of all the lands where people live. You will see the high peaks of the mountains, the wide valleys, the deep seas, and the many rivers that flow across the earth. This will help you understand what you are leaving behind and the new destiny that awaits you.

But this will not happen immediately. You have forty days before this takes place.

During these days, go back to your people and teach them everything you can. Share wisdom and guidance with them, so they may turn their hearts toward the path of life. Teach them urgently, because the knowledge you give them will help them survive in the last days and avoid destruction. It will prepare them to live righteously in the time to come, when my glory is fully revealed."

Chapter 77

Then I, Baruch, left that place and gathered all the people together. I called everyone, from the most important to the least, so that they could hear my words. When they had all come, I spoke to them:

"Listen carefully, people of Israel, and think about the situation you are in. Look at how few of you remain from the twelve tribes. Once, we were a great nation, but now only a small group is left. The Lord gave His law to you and your ancestors, setting you apart from all the other nations. This law was your guide, a promise of righteousness, and the path to life.

But your brothers, the other tribes, disobeyed the commandments of the Most High, and He judged them fairly. He did not spare the first tribes that sinned, and He did not overlook the ones that came after.

They were all taken away into exile, and none of them remained. Now, look at yourselves—you are still here with me because of His mercy.

So I urge you, follow the right path before the Lord. If you return to His commandments and live righteously, you will not suffer the same fate as your brothers. Instead, those who were scattered will come back to you. The Mighty One, whom you serve, is merciful and kind. The One you trust is full of grace and truth. He wants to bless you, not harm you.

Have you not seen what happened to Zion? Do you think the city itself committed a sin, and that is why it was destroyed? Do you believe the land itself did something wrong and was punished? No, you must understand this: Zion was innocent, but it was destroyed because of your sins and the sins of your brothers. Because some turned away from the right path, Zion, which had remained faithful, was handed over to its enemies."

When I finished speaking, the people all responded together:

"We remember, as much as we can, the great things the Mighty One has done for us and our ancestors. And for what we do not remember, we trust in His mercy, for He knows everything. But before you leave us, Baruch, we ask one thing: Write a letter of instruction and hope for our brothers in Babel. Strengthen them with your words, just as you have strengthened us. The leaders of Israel have been taken away from us, the lights that once guided us have gone out, and the wells from which we once drank have dried up. We feel lost, like wanderers in a forest or travelers in a desert."

I answered them:

"Do not lose hope, because the leaders, the lamps, and the fountains all come from the law. Even though I am leaving, the law will remain with you forever. If you focus on it and commit yourselves to its wisdom, you will always have light to guide your path, a leader to show you the way, and a source of life to sustain you.

But because you have asked me, I will write to your brothers in Babel to give them words of hope and guidance. I will also send a letter to the nine and a half tribes scattered in distant lands. One letter will be delivered by messengers, and the other I will send through a bird so that my words may reach them all."

So on the twenty-first day of the eighth month, I sat alone under the shade of an oak tree. In the quiet, I wrote two letters. One I gave to three men to take to those in Babel, and the other I gave to an eagle to carry to the nine and a half tribes living beyond the Euphrates River.

I spoke to the eagle, saying:

"You, noble bird, were created by the Most High to soar above all others. Now, I command you in His name to take this letter and deliver it quickly. Do not rest in a nest or perch on a tree until you have flown across the great waters of the Euphrates and reached the people to whom this message is sent.

Remember, it was a dove that brought back the olive branch to Noah, showing that peace had come after the flood. Ravens were sent to feed Elijah when he was in need. Even King Solomon, in his wisdom, sent birds to deliver his messages, and they obeyed him.

Now, do not hesitate or turn aside from your mission. Fly straight and fast, carrying out the command of the Mighty One, just as I have instructed you, so that His plan may be fulfilled through you."

With that, the eagle spread its wings and took flight, carrying the letter high above the earth. Meanwhile, I entrusted the other letter to the messengers headed for Babel. In this way, I made sure that the words of hope and instruction would reach all the scattered children of Israel.

Chapter 78~81

This is the letter that Baruch, the son of Neriah, wrote to the nine and a half tribes who were taken into exile and now live beyond the great Euphrates River. These are the words he sent to them:

"This is the message from Baruch, the son of Neriah, to my brothers who have been taken far from home. May grace and peace be with you from the Most High, who created us all and has never stopped loving us. From the very beginning, He has shown His love for us, even when we turned away from Him. He has never hated us, but like a caring father, He has disciplined us to lead us back to the right path.

I know this is true: even though we are scattered and living in different lands, we are still one people. We are all descendants of the twelve tribes of Israel, united by the covenant we made with our one true God. We share the same ancestors and, because of that, the same destiny.

Because of this, I have made sure to write this letter to you before my time comes to an end. I hope my words bring you comfort as you face the struggles that have come upon you. I also hope they remind you to grieve for the suffering of our brothers who are going through the same trials. Most of all, I want you to understand that our exile was not unfair or random—it was a just judgment. What has happened to us is less than what we actually deserved for turning away from the commandments of the Mighty One. But through this judgment, we have been given a chance to be worthy of the promises made to our ancestors for the future.

If you realize that the suffering we face now is meant to save us from being condemned in the end, then you will find a new kind of hope—one that lasts forever. But this hope requires action. You must turn away from the idols and false beliefs that led you away from the truth. If you do this, the Most High will remember you. He is the same God who made an eternal promise to our forefathers, vowing never to abandon or forget their descendants. Because of His great mercy, He will gather all of us who have been scattered and bring us back together.

Now, my brothers, think about what happened to Zion. Nebuchadnezzar, the king of Babel, came with his armies—not because Zion itself had sinned, but because we, its people, had turned away from the Most High. We failed to keep the commandments He gave us. Yet even in His judgment, He has been merciful, punishing us far less than we deserved.

When the enemy surrounded Jerusalem, messengers from the Most High came to act. They tore down parts of the city's strong defenses and destroyed the iron fortifications that seemed impossible to break. But at the same time, they made sure to protect some of the sacred objects from the temple, hiding them so the enemy would not defile them. After that, they left the city's walls broken, the house of the Lord raided, and the temple burned, so that our enemies would not claim victory by their own strength.

Despite this destruction, our brothers were taken away to live in exile in Babel, far from the land of their ancestors. Those of us who remain are only a small group. This is the suffering I write to you about. I know how much comfort Zion once brought you. Just knowing that your brothers were safe in their land gave you peace, even though you had been taken far away.

But now, I want to share a message of hope. I, too, mourned for Zion. In my sorrow, I begged the Most High for mercy. I cried out to Him, asking if this suffering would last forever and if these troubles would ever come to an end.

The Mighty One, in His endless grace and kindness, heard my prayer. He sent me words of comfort to ease my pain and gave me visions to replace my despair with hope. In His mercy, He allowed me to understand the mysteries of time and revealed what will happen in the future.

So, my brothers, do not lose heart. The suffering we face now is not the end—it is only part of a greater plan. The Most High, whose wisdom and kindness go beyond what we can understand, has already prepared what comes next. Hold on to His law and the promises He gave our ancestors, because the days of restoration and glory are coming soon."

Chapter 82~84

My dear brothers, I am writing to you so that you may find comfort during these difficult times. Take courage, knowing that the Creator, who rules everything with justice, will bring judgment on our enemies. He will repay them for the wrongs they have done to us, for the evil they have spread, and for how they have ignored His laws. Also, remember that the time the Most High has planned is coming closer, and His mercy is reaching out to us. His final judgment is near, and when it comes, everything that has been broken will be restored.

Look around and see what is happening even now. The nations of the world seem to be thriving, yet they continue to do evil, piling sin upon sin. But their success will not last—it will disappear like smoke in the air. We see their power and arrogance as they refuse to honor the Mighty One, but their strength is as small as a drop of water, quickly gone. They may act as if they can resist the laws of the Most High, but in the end, they will be as insignificant as dust.

Think about the way they proudly display their wealth and power while ignoring the commandments of the Mighty One. Their riches and glory will fade away like mist, leaving nothing behind. Consider their beauty, which is covered in sin and wrongdoing—it will wither as quickly as dry grass in the scorching sun. Their cruelty and oppression may seem unstoppable, but like waves crashing on the shore, they will break and disappear.

And what about their pride? They lift themselves up, bragging about the power they have been given, yet they refuse to acknowledge the One who gave it to them. Their arrogance will vanish like a cloud blown away by the wind, leaving no trace behind.

The Most High will not wait forever. He will bring about His plan at the right time. He will judge everyone who lives on this earth. Every action, every sin, and even the hidden thoughts deep in people's hearts will be revealed. Nothing will remain secret—everything will come to light before all, and those who are guilty will be held responsible.

So do not let what you see now make you lose hope. Instead, hold on to faith and trust that the promises of the Most High will come true. Do not focus on the temporary success of the nations that seem to be thriving now. Instead, remember the inheritance that has been promised to us in the end. The pleasures of this world will disappear like shadows, but the reward waiting for us is eternal.

The end of this age is coming quickly, and everything in it will pass away. When this time is over, the great power of the Mighty One will be revealed for all to see, as everything is judged. On that day, His righteousness will be shown clearly, and the sins of the nations will no longer be hidden. Then, His everlasting kingdom will shine in full glory, unshaken and eternal. Let this be the hope that carries us through every trial.

So, my brothers, I am writing to encourage you to stay strong in your faith. Hold on tightly to what you have learned so that you do not lose everything—both in this life and in the next. Think about this: everything that exists now, everything that has already happened, and everything that will come in the future—none of it is completely good or completely bad. Life is always changing, reminding us that nothing stays the same forever.

Good health eventually turns into sickness. Strength fades into weakness. Power never lasts and will one day disappear. Even the energy of youth will one day give way to old age and, finally, to the end of life itself.

Beauty and grace, which people celebrate, will eventually fade, leaving only decay behind. The innocence of childhood, full of promise, often turns into disappointment and shame. Honor and glory, no matter how great, will one day be forgotten. Happiness, no matter how bright, will eventually turn into sadness.

Even the loudest voices of pride will be silenced, crumbling into dust. Riches and possessions, which seem so secure, cannot stop the reality of death. Desires that control and consume people will lead only to an end they cannot escape. Pleasure that seems enjoyable for a moment will bring judgment later.

Lies and falsehoods may seem to win for a time, but they will always be exposed in the end. Sweet words that once comforted will turn bitter when the truth is revealed. Friendships that are not built on honesty will eventually break, turning into betrayal.

Since we already see these things happening, do you really think they will go unnoticed? When everything reaches its end, every hidden truth will be brought into the light.

Now, listen carefully. While I am still with you, I am sharing this wisdom. More than anything, I urge you to follow the commandments of the Mighty One. Before I leave this world, I want to remind you of His instructions so that you can live by them.

Remember what Moses did long ago. He called on heaven and earth to witness his words when he warned the people, saying, "If you disobey the law, you will be scattered, but if you follow it, you will be blessed and grow strong." He spoke these words when all twelve tribes were still together in the wilderness. But after he died, you turned away from his teachings, and because of that, everything he warned about has now happened.

Now I speak to you after all your suffering. Moses warned you before these troubles came, and his words came true because you abandoned the law. In the same way, I now tell you this: If you listen and follow the teachings I give you, the Mighty One will bless you with all the good things He has prepared for you.

Let this letter be a witness between us. Let it remind you of the commandments of the Mighty One, and let it stand as my defense before Him. Never forget Zion, the law, the holy land, your brothers, the covenant, or your ancestors. Keep the festivals and the Sabbaths. Pass this letter down to your children, just as your ancestors passed down the law to you.

Always seek the Mighty One with all your heart and soul. Pray sincerely and ask for His mercy, so that He does not count all your sins against you. Instead, may He remember your honesty and your desire to follow Him. Teach your children to do the same, so they can walk in His ways and receive the blessings He has promised to those who remain faithful.

If our Creator does not judge us with mercy, then we are all truly hopeless. This life is short, and everything we love will one day fade away. Do not fool yourselves into thinking that your actions—whether good or bad—will go unnoticed. The Mighty One sees everything, even the hidden thoughts of the heart and the deepest secrets of the soul. Nothing is hidden from Him; everything will be revealed when the time of judgment comes.

Think about how short life is. No matter how strong a person is, sickness and weakness will eventually come. Youthful energy fades into old age. Power and influence do not last forever—they always disappear with time. Beauty, no matter how admired, will one day fade into ruin.

Many chase after wealth and status, but these things do not last. Pride turns into humiliation, and those who once had great honor will eventually be forgotten. Riches disappear, and the happiness people seek in them will eventually be replaced with sorrow. Even the loudest and most powerful voices will one day be silent, and no amount of wealth can keep someone from the grave.

People chase after their desires, but in the end, all of it leads to death. Those who live only for pleasure will one day face judgment. Lies and deceit may work for a while, but eventually, the truth will be revealed, and they will be condemned. Friendships built on dishonesty will crumble, leaving only betrayal and pain.

Do you really think that all these things will go unpunished? When everything comes to an end, the truth will be made clear, and every action will be judged. The Mighty One will bring His time of judgment quickly, and everything will happen just as He has planned. He will judge the world with perfect justice, and nothing will be hidden from Him. Every secret thought and every hidden deed will be brought into the light.

So do not put your hope in the temporary pleasures of this world. Instead, focus on what has been promised to us—the eternal inheritance that awaits those who remain faithful. When the end of this age comes, the great power of the Mighty One will be revealed. On the day of judgment, all creation will see His justice. Let us prepare our hearts now and live by His commandments, so that we may stand before Him blameless and receive His mercy and grace.

Chapter 85~87

In the past, our ancestors had righteous leaders—prophets and holy men who stood between us and the Mighty One. These faithful people guided us and prayed on our behalf when we failed. Because of their goodness and strong faith, the Mighty One heard their prayers and forgave our mistakes. Their prayers cleansed us and brought us back into His favor.

But now, things are different. Those righteous people have passed away, and the prophets who spoke the words of the Most High are no longer with us. We have been taken from our land, and Zion, our sacred home, has been taken from us. All that remains is the Mighty One and His holy law. Yet even in this time of loss, we still have hope, because His law is our guide and proof of His promise to us.

If we fully turn back to Him and live according to His commandments, He will not only return what we lost, but He will give us something far greater than we can imagine. What we lost was temporary—it could be destroyed or taken away. But what the Mighty

One will give us in return will last forever. It is a promise that should strengthen us and keep our faith strong.

That is why I have also written to our brothers in Babel, so they too may understand these truths and find comfort. Keep these words in your hearts, because we are still under the mercy and freedom that the Most High has given us. He is patient and kind, showing us what is coming and helping us prepare for the future. This is a great gift, giving us the chance to be ready.

Before the day of judgment arrives and the truth is revealed to all, we must prepare ourselves. Let us hold on to hope instead of falling into despair. Let us seek eternal peace with our ancestors instead of facing suffering with those who rejected the ways of the Mighty One. The strength of this world is fading, and time is running out. The final moments are approaching, and the end of the journey is near.

So be ready, just as travelers prepare for the last part of their trip. When you leave this life, may you find peace and not punishment. The Mighty One will fulfill everything that has been foretold. When that time comes, there will be no more chances to repent, no more moments of mercy, and no more opportunities to pray for forgiveness. Love offerings will cease, cries for help will go unanswered, and no prophets or righteous people will be left to speak for us. The time to act will be over, and only judgment will remain.

On that day, those who lived in corruption will face destruction, cast into fire and eternal judgment. The world follows one law, given by One Creator, and in the end, everyone will face the same decision. The Mighty One will separate the righteous from the wicked. Those who can be forgiven will be saved and purified, but those who refuse to change will be cast away.

When you receive this letter, read it carefully when you gather together, and reflect on its words, especially during times of fasting. Let it remind you of the covenant and encourage you to stay strong. Remember me, as I also remember you, and let this letter keep us connected in shared faith and hope.

This is the end of the letter of Baruch, son of Neriah.

After writing these words, I folded and sealed the letter. Then, I tied it securely to the neck of an eagle and released it into the sky, sending it to our brothers far away. And so, I entrusted these words to their journey, hoping they would bring guidance, comfort, and hope to all who received them.

The Third Book of Baruch

Chapter One

I, Baruch, was deeply troubled and filled with sorrow as I thought about the suffering of my people. My heart ached, and I mourned over how King Nebuchadnezzar had been allowed by the Almighty to destroy the holy city. I struggled to understand why this had happened to us. Crying out, I said, "Lord, why did you allow your vineyard to be ruined? Why have you let it be destroyed? Why did you punish us in this way instead of disciplining us differently? Instead, you handed us over to these nations that now mock us, saying, 'Where is their God?'"

As these thoughts overwhelmed me, tears streamed down my face, and my heart grew heavier with sorrow. But as I wept, pouring out my grief, a vision appeared before me. I saw an angel of the Lord descending with a bright and powerful presence. He came near and spoke to me, saying, "Man of God, greatly loved, do not let your heart be so burdened over the fate of Jerusalem. Listen to the words of the Almighty, for He has sent me to reveal His divine plan to you."

The angel continued, "This is what the Lord God Almighty says: Your prayer has been heard, Baruch. The Most High has received your cries and your sorrow. He has seen the pain in your heart and has listened to your words."

Hearing this, I began to feel a sense of calm, though my mind was still filled with questions. The angel, sensing my uncertainty, said, "Do not trouble yourself by trying to understand everything right now. The ways of God are beyond what you can see. I have been sent to show you things far greater than what you have asked. These are truths beyond your understanding at this moment."

With deep respect, I replied, "As surely as the Lord lives, I will not question or complain if you reveal these mysteries to me. And if I fail to keep this promise, may God judge me on the day of reckoning."

Then the angel, speaking with both authority and kindness, said, "Come, Baruch. Follow me, and I will show you the hidden and sacred things of the Most High. Open your heart to receive these truths, for they will bring light to your soul and wisdom to your spirit."

At that moment, I resolved to listen, ready to receive the knowledge that the Lord was about to reveal through His messenger. My sorrow began to change into anticipation as I followed the angel, preparing to understand the deep and eternal wisdom of the Almighty.

Chapter Two

The angel took me with him to where the heavens were firmly set in place. There, I saw an enormous river—so wide that no one could cross it, not even the foreign nations that God had created. Then, he led me further and took me up to the first heaven, where we arrived at a massive door. He turned to me and said, "Let's go inside."

As we entered, it felt as if we were flying, traveling a distance that would have taken thirty days to walk.

Inside, I saw a vast plain stretching across the heaven. There were beings living there, but they looked different from humans. Their faces resembled cattle, they had horns like deer, feet like goats, and their lower bodies were covered in wool like sheep.

I, Baruch, turned to the angel and asked, "Please tell me, how thick is this heaven we passed through? How wide is it? And what is this plain you have shown me? I want to share this with the people on earth."

The angel, whose name was Phamael, answered, "The door you saw is the gateway to heaven. Its thickness is as great as the distance from earth to heaven, and the width of the plain you saw is just as vast."

Then the angel said, "Come with me, and I will show you even greater mysteries."

I asked him, "Please tell me, who are these people?"

He replied, "They are the ones who built the great tower, trying to fight against God. Because of their actions, the Lord removed them from the earth."

Chapter Three

The angel of the Lord took me up to the second heaven and showed me a door that looked just like the first one. He said, "Let's go inside." So we entered, traveling as if we were flying, covering a distance that would take sixty days to walk.

Inside, I saw another vast plain, and it was filled with people. But their appearance was strange—they had faces like dogs and feet like deer.

I asked the angel, "Who are these people?"

He answered, "These are the ones who planned to build the great tower. They forced many men and women to make bricks for the construction. Among them was a woman who was forced to keep working even while she was giving birth. They did not allow her to stop, so she gave birth while making bricks. She wrapped her baby in her cloak and continued working.

When the Lord appeared to them, He confused their languages. By that time, they had already built the tower up to a height of 463 cubits. Then they took a tool and tried to drill through the sky, saying, 'Let's see if heaven is made of clay, copper, or iron.'

When God saw what they were doing, He did not let them continue. Instead, He struck them with blindness and caused their speech to become confused. That is why they are as you see them now."

Chapter Four

I, Baruch, said, "Lord, you have already shown me incredible and amazing things. Now, I ask you, for the Lord's sake, to show me everything else."

The angel replied, "Come, let's go further." We traveled together, covering a distance that would take about 185 days to walk.

He led me to a vast plain where I saw a massive serpent that looked like it was made of stone. Then, he showed me Hades, a place that was dark, empty, and unclean.

I asked, "What is this dragon, and what is the creature surrounding it?"

The angel explained, "This dragon devours the bodies of those who lived wicked lives. It feeds on them. Hades works the same way—it consumes and never stops. Each day, it takes about a cubit of water from the sea, yet the sea never runs dry."

I asked, "How is that possible?"

The angel said, "Listen carefully. The Lord created 360 rivers, and the three largest ones are the Alphias, the Aburos, and the Gerikos. These rivers constantly flow into the sea, keeping it from ever running out."

Then I said, "Please show me the tree that caused Adam to go astray."

The angel answered, "That tree is actually a vine, planted by the angel Samail. It made the Lord angry, and He cursed both Samail and the vine. That's why God commanded Adam not to touch it. The devil, out of jealousy, used it to deceive Adam."

I asked, "If the vine was so dangerous and brought a curse upon Adam, why does it still serve an important purpose today?"

The angel replied, "That is a good question. When God sent the flood to destroy all living things, including 409,000 giants, the water rose 15 cubits above the highest mountains. The flood reached Paradise and wiped out every plant and flower. However, a small branch of the vine was carried by the waters and left on the earth.

"When the flood ended and the land appeared again, Noah came out of the ark and began planting everything he found. Among them, he discovered the vine branch. He wasn't sure what it was and prayed for guidance. That's when I came to him and explained its origin.

"Noah asked, 'Should I plant this, or should I destroy it? Since Adam was cursed because of it, will I also bring God's anger upon myself if I plant it?' He was unsure, so he prayed for forty days, pleading with God to tell him what to do.

"Finally, God sent the angel Sarasel with a message. The angel told Noah, 'Plant the vine. The Lord says this: What was once bitter will become sweet, what was cursed will become a blessing, and its fruit will represent the blood of God. Just as humanity was condemned through it, through Jesus Christ, Emmanuel, it will now offer a way back into Paradise.'

"Remember this, Baruch: Just as Adam was cursed and lost God's glory because of this vine, people today also fall further from God when they drink too much wine. By overindulging, they bring judgment upon themselves and prepare for eternal punishment.

"Nothing good comes from drinking in excess. Those who drink too much commit terrible sins: brothers turn against brothers, fathers lose compassion for their sons, children stop respecting their parents, and because of drunkenness, all kinds of evil arise—murder, adultery, immorality, lying, stealing, and many other sins. Truly, no good comes from it."

I, Baruch, said, "Lord, you have already shown me amazing and powerful things. Now, I ask you, for the sake of the Lord, to show me everything else."

The angel replied, "Come, let's go further." We traveled together, covering a distance that would take about 185 days to walk.

He led me to a vast plain where I saw a huge serpent that looked as if it were made of stone. Then, he showed me Hades—a dark, empty, and unclean place.

I asked, "What is this dragon, and what is the creature surrounding it?"

The angel explained, "This dragon feeds on the bodies of those who lived sinful lives. It grows stronger by consuming them. Hades works the same way—it takes from the world, but never runs out. Every day, it absorbs a cubit of water from the sea, yet the sea never shrinks."

I asked, "How is that possible?"

The angel said, "Listen carefully. The Lord created 360 rivers, and the three largest ones are the Alphias, the Aburos, and the Gerikos.

These rivers flow constantly into the sea, keeping it from ever running dry."

Then I said, "Please show me the tree that led Adam astray."

The angel answered, "That tree is actually a vine, planted by the angel Samail. It angered the Lord, and He cursed both Samail and the vine. That is why God commanded Adam not to touch it. The devil, out of jealousy, used it to deceive Adam."

I asked, "If this vine caused such harm and was cursed by God, why does it still have such an important purpose?"

The angel replied, "That is a good question. When God sent the great flood to destroy all living things, including 409,000 giants, the water rose 15 cubits above the highest mountains. The flood even reached Paradise, wiping out every plant and flower. However, a small branch of the vine was carried by the waters and left on the earth.

"When the flood ended and the land reappeared, Noah left the ark and began planting the things he found. Among them, he discovered the vine branch. He was unsure what it was and prayed for guidance. That's when I came to him and explained its origin.

"Noah asked, 'Should I plant this, or should I destroy it? Since Adam was cursed because of it, will I also bring God's anger upon myself if I plant it?' He was uncertain, so he prayed for forty days, asking God to tell him what to do.

"Finally, God sent the angel Sarasel with a message. The angel told Noah, 'Plant the vine. The Lord says this: What was once bitter will become sweet, what was cursed will become a blessing, and its fruit will represent the blood of God. Just as humanity was condemned through it, through Jesus Christ, Emmanuel, it will now offer a way back into Paradise.'

"Remember this, Baruch: Just as Adam was cursed and lost God's glory because of this vine, people today also fall further from God when they drink too much wine. By overindulging, they bring judgment upon themselves and prepare for eternal punishment.

"Nothing good comes from drinking excessively. Those who do become reckless and commit terrible sins: brothers turn against brothers, fathers lose compassion for their children, children stop respecting their parents, and because of drunkenness, all kinds of evil arise—murder, adultery, immorality, lying, stealing, and many other wrongs. Truly, nothing good comes from it."

Chapter Five

I, Baruch, turned to the angel and asked, "Lord, may I ask you something?"

The angel replied, "Ask whatever you wish."

I continued, "You told me that the serpent drinks a cubit of water from the sea each day. Can you tell me how big its stomach is?"

The angel answered, "Its stomach is as large as Hades itself. It is so massive that it stretches as far as a group of 300 men could throw a heavy stone."

Then he said, "Come with me, and I will show you things even greater than this."

Chapter Six

The angel took me to the place where the sun rises.

He showed me a chariot pulled by four horses, with fire blazing beneath it. A man sat on the chariot, wearing a crown made of flames.

Around the chariot stood forty angels, and in front of it ran a massive bird—so large that it looked as big as nine mountains.

I asked the angel, "What is this bird?"

He answered, "This is the guardian of the world."

I asked again, "How does this bird protect the world? Please explain it to me."

The angel said, "This bird travels with the sun as it moves. It spreads its wings to absorb the sun's fiery rays. If it didn't do this, the heat would be too strong, and no living creature—human or animal—would survive. That is why God created this bird for this purpose."

Then the bird spread its wings, and I saw large letters written on its right wing. The letters covered a huge space, about the size of a threshing floor, around 4,000 measures wide. They shined like gold.

The angel said, "Read what is written."

So I read the letters, and they said: "Neither the earth nor the heavens can hold me, but the wings of fire carry me."

I asked the angel, "What is the name of this bird?"

He replied, "It is called the Phoenix."

I asked, "What does it eat?"

He answered, "It feeds on manna from heaven and the dew of the earth."

I asked again, "Does it produce waste?"

The angel replied, "Yes, it excretes a worm, and from this, cinnamon is formed. This cinnamon is used by kings and rulers. But wait, and you will see the glory of God."

While the angel was still speaking, a sudden thunderclap shook the ground beneath us.

I asked, "What is this sound?"

The angel explained, "The angels are opening the 365 gates of heaven, allowing light to separate from darkness."

Then I heard a voice say, "Light-giver, bring splendor to the world!"

At that moment, I also heard the bird's call and asked, "What is that sound?"

The angel answered, "This is the cry that wakes the roosters on earth. Just as people signal each other, the rooster announces the start of the day. As the angels prepare the sun, the rooster crows to let the earth know morning has come."

Chapter Seven

I asked, "Where does the sun begin its journey after the rooster crows?"

The angel replied, "Listen, Baruch, everything I have shown you so far is within the first and second heavens. But in the third heaven, the sun moves through and spreads its light across the world. Be patient, and you will see the glory of God."

As the angel spoke, I saw the bird appear again. At first, it looked small, but it grew larger and larger until it returned to its full size.

Following the bird, I saw the sun shining brightly, surrounded by angels who carried it. A magnificent crown rested on the sun, and its light was so intense that we couldn't look directly at it.

At the same moment, the phoenix spread its wings wide. The brilliance of the scene was overwhelming, and I was filled with such fear that I turned away and hid under the angel's wings.

The angel reassured me, saying, "Do not be afraid, Baruch. Stay here, and soon you will see the sun as it sets."

Chapter Eight

He led me toward the west, and as the sun neared the horizon, I once again saw the great bird flying ahead, guiding the sun. The sun followed closely behind, surrounded by angels. When it reached its resting place, I watched as the angels removed the crown from its head. The bird, exhausted from its journey, let its wings droop as if weighed down by fatigue.

Curious about what I had seen, I asked, "Why do the angels take the crown off the sun's head? And why does the bird look so tired?"

The angel explained, "At the end of each day, four angels carry the sun's crown to heaven so that it can be renewed. This is necessary because, as the sun travels over the earth, its rays and crown become tainted. Each day, they must be cleansed and restored."

I then asked, "How do the sun's rays become unclean?"

The angel replied, "As the sun shines on the earth, it witnesses the sins of humanity. These include acts of immorality, stealing, violence, idolatry, drunkenness, murder, jealousy, gossip, deceit, and many other things that offend God. Because of this, the sun's light becomes stained and must be purified daily."

Wanting to understand more, I asked, "Why is the bird so worn out?"

The angel answered, "The bird is exhausted because it spends the entire day protecting the earth from the full heat of the sun. It spreads its wings to absorb the intense rays so that they don't burn everything below. Without its constant effort, as I told you before, no living thing would be able to survive the sun's scorching heat."

Chapter Nine

When night arrived, the moon and stars appeared in the sky. I, Baruch, turned to the angel and asked, "Lord, please explain this to me as well. Where does the moon go when it disappears, and what path does it follow?"

The angel replied, "Be patient, and soon you will see and understand."

The next day, I saw the moon. It looked like a woman seated in a chariot with wheels. In front of the chariot were oxen and lambs, and many angels traveled alongside it.

I asked, "Lord, what are the oxen and lambs?"

The angel answered, "These are also angels."

I then asked, "Why does the moon sometimes appear larger and at other times smaller?"

The angel explained, "Listen, Baruch. The moon was created by God to be beautiful and unique. However, during Adam's first sin, the moon gave its light to Samael when he took the form of the serpent. Instead of hiding its brightness, it shined even more. This angered God, so He reduced its light and shortened its days."

I asked, "Why doesn't the moon shine all the time, but only at night?"

The angel replied, "Just as servants do not speak freely in the presence of a king, the moon and stars cannot shine in the presence of the sun. The stars remain in their places, but their light is overpowered by the sun's brightness. Meanwhile, the moon is safe, but its light fades because of the sun's intense heat and brilliance."

Chapter Ten

After the archangel had taught me all these things, he led me to the third heaven. There, I saw a vast, endless plain, and in the center was a peaceful lake of clear water. Surrounding the lake were many birds of all kinds, but they were unlike any birds I had ever seen on earth. Among them, I noticed a crane as large as an ox. All of the birds were magnificent, far greater than anything found in the world below.

I turned to the angel and asked, "What is this plain? What is this lake? And why are so many birds gathered around it?"

The angel replied, "Listen carefully, Baruch. This plain, which holds many hidden mysteries, is where the souls of the righteous come together. Here, they live in peace and form choirs to praise the Lord."

He continued, "The water in this lake is what the clouds draw up to bring rain to the earth. That rain helps plants grow and produce fruit."

I then asked, "And what about these birds?"

The angel answered, "These birds never stop singing praises to the Lord."

I, Baruch, then said, "Lord, why do people say that rain comes from the sea?"

The angel explained, "Some rain does come from the sea and from water sources on the earth. But the rain that helps crops grow comes from this place. From now on, understand that what people call the 'dew of heaven' also comes from here."

Chapter Eleven

The angel led me from that place to the fifth heaven. When we arrived, I saw that the gate was closed. I asked, "Lord, will the gate be opened so we can enter?"

The angel replied, "We cannot go in until Michael, the one who holds the keys to heaven, arrives. Be patient, and you will see the glory of God."

Suddenly, a loud noise like thunder filled the air. I asked, "Lord, what is that sound?"

The angel answered, "It is the archangel Michael descending to collect the prayers of people on earth."

Then a voice called out, "Let the gate be opened!" At that moment, the gate swung open with a sound as powerful as a thunderclap.

Michael appeared, and the angel with me stepped forward, bowing low and saying, "Greetings, commander of all the heavenly armies."

Michael replied, "Greetings to you as well, our brother and messenger of God's revelations to the righteous."

After they exchanged greetings, they stood together. Then, I saw Michael holding a massive bowl. It was so large that its depth stretched from heaven to earth, and its width reached from north to south.

Amazed, I asked, "Lord, what is that bowl that the archangel Michael is carrying?"

The angel answered, "This bowl holds the virtues and good deeds of the righteous. Michael gathers them and presents them before God in heaven."

Chapter Twelve

As I was speaking with them, I saw angels approaching, each carrying baskets filled with beautiful flowers. They brought these baskets to Michael and handed them over. Curious, I turned to the angel beside me and asked, "Lord, who are these angels, and what are they carrying?"

He answered, "These are the angels responsible for overseeing different regions and nations."

I watched as Michael took the baskets from the angels and emptied the flowers into the large bowl he was holding. Then, the angel explained, "The flowers being poured into the bowl represent the good deeds and virtues of the righteous."

As I looked closer, I noticed other angels arriving, but their baskets were not completely full. These angels seemed troubled and hesitant, standing back instead of stepping forward. It was clear they hadn't gathered enough to fill their baskets.

Michael saw their hesitation and called out, "Come forward, you angels, and bring whatever you have collected."

They obeyed, but as they poured what little they had into the bowl, both Michael and the angel beside me looked deeply saddened. The contributions from these angels were not enough to fill the bowl completely.

Chapter Thirteen

Then, more angels arrived, crying and trembling with fear. They said, "Look at us, Lord! We have become stained and darkened because we were assigned to serve evil people. Please, we beg you, remove us from their presence."

Michael replied, "You cannot leave them, for we must not let the enemy claim victory. But tell me, what do you wish?"

The angels answered, "Michael, our commander, we ask you to take us away from them. We can no longer bear being among these wicked and corrupt people. They have no goodness in them—only greed and wrongdoing.

"We have never seen them enter a place of worship, seek guidance from spiritual leaders, or do anything righteous. Instead, wherever there is murder, they are involved. Wherever there is immorality, theft, lies, jealousy, drunkenness, violence, or idolatry, they are at the center of it all. Their actions are evil, and they continue in their wickedness without regret. Please, release us from them."

Michael turned to them and said, "Wait here while I seek the Lord's will to find out what should be done."

Chapter Fourteen

At that moment, Michael left, and the large doors closed tightly behind him. A deep, powerful sound, like rolling thunder, echoed through the heavens.

I turned to the angel beside me and asked, "What is that loud noise?"

The angel replied, "That is Michael presenting the good deeds of people before God."

Chapter Fifteen

At that moment, Michael returned, and the gate opened. He carried oil with him.

For the angels who had brought full baskets, he filled them with oil and said, "Take this and give a hundredfold reward to our friends—those who have worked hard and done good. Those who have planted well will harvest well."

To the angels who had brought half-filled baskets, he said, "Come and receive your reward based on what you brought, and deliver it to the people on earth."

Then, speaking to both groups—the ones with full baskets and those with half-filled ones—he said, "Go and bless our friends. Tell them that the Lord says: 'You have been faithful with little, so I will give you even more. Enter into the joy of the Lord.'"

Chapter Sixteen

Then he turned to those who had brought nothing and said, "Do not be sad, and do not weep, but do not abandon the people on earth either.

Since they have angered me with their actions, go and make them jealous. Stir their frustration and turn their hearts against those who are not even a nation, against people who lack understanding.

Send swarms of caterpillars and locusts, rust and grasshoppers. Strike them with hail, lightning, and fury. Bring punishment through the sword and death, and send demons to trouble their children.

For they refused to listen to my voice. They ignored my commands and did not follow them. Instead, they rejected my instructions, turned away from my places of worship, and insulted the priests who spoke my words to them."

Chapter Seventeen

As he finished speaking, the door closed, and we stepped away.

The angel then led me back to the place where my journey had first begun.

When I came to my senses, I praised God for allowing me to witness such incredible things.

And to you, my brothers who read these revelations, give glory to God, so that He may also honor us—now and forever, for all eternity! Amen.

Thank You for Reading

Dear Reader,

We hope this timeless classic has sparked your imagination and enriched your literary journey. Now that you've turned the final page, we want to share a vision for the future of reading—one where every classic you've ever wanted to explore is at your fingertips, in a format that best suits your life.

We'd like to invite you to gain immediate, unlimited digital & audiobook access to hundreds of the most treasured literary classics ever written—along with the option to secure deluxe paperback, hardcover & box set editions at printing cost. Together, we can spark a new global literary renaissance alongside our small, independent publishing house called "The Library of Alexandria."

Thousands of years ago, the Library of Alexandria stood as a beacon of knowledge—until it was lost to history. We aim to reignite that spirit of preservation and discovery right now, in the modern age—only this time, it's accessible to all, in every language and every format.

Picture a world where every timeless classic, novel, poem, or philosophical treatise is not only available to read but also updated for today's readers—modernized, translated into any language or dialect, and ready to enjoy in any format you choose, whether that is in an eBook, audiobook, paperback, or deluxe hardcover & box set version a printing cost.

By joining our movement to rebuild the modern Library of Alexandria, you become part of an unprecedented mission to offer:

- **Unlimited Audiobook & eBook Access to the Greatest Classics of All Time**

  Instantly explore thousands of legendary works, from Plato and Shakespeare to Jane Austen and Leo Tolstoy. All are instantly ready to read or listen to, giving you a complete literary universe at your fingertips.

- **Paperback & Deluxe Editions at Printing Costs:**

  Purchase any title in a paperback, deluxe hardbound, or deluxe boxset edition at printing costs, shipped right to your doorstep. Curate your personal library of Alexandria with editions worthy of display—crafted to last, designed to captivate, and delivered straight to your door.

- **Modern translations for Contemporary Readers in all languages and dialects**

  Discover a vast selection of classics reimagined in clear, current language—no more struggling with outdated phrases or obscure references. Next to the original versions, we aim to offer translations in as many languages and dialects as possible.

  As we continue our translation efforts and add new languages, readers everywhere can connect with these works as if they were written today. By bridging linguistic divides, you're contributing to ensuring that these timeless stories become more meaningful, accessible, and inspiring for people across the globe.

- **Your Personal Library of Alexandria:**

  Over the months and years, you'll curate a unique physical archive of classics—each volume a testament to your taste, curiosity, and love of knowledge. It's not just about owning books—it's about curating a cultural legacy you'll cherish and pass down for generations to come.

- **Join a Global Literary Renaissance:**

    Your support fuels an ongoing mission: allowing us to reinvest in offering deluxe print editions (including special boxsets) at their true cost, broaden the range of available formats and translations, and extend the reach of these works to new audiences worldwide. By joining today, you're not just preserving a legacy of masterpieces; you set in motion a powerful wave of literary accessibility.

    We are more than a publisher—we're a movement, and we can't do it alone. Your support lets us scale our mission, preserving and reimagining history's greatest works for tomorrow's readers.

Become a Torchbearer of knowledge.

Thank you for picking up this book and allowing us into your literary journey. As you turn the pages, know that you're part of something larger: a global effort to keep these stories alive, share their wisdom across borders and generations, and spark a true cultural revival for the modern era.

If this resonates with you—please consider taking the next step by visiting:

www.libraryofalexandria.com

With gratitude and a shared love of knowledge,

The Modern Library of Alexandria Team

Visit:

www.libraryofalexandria.com

Or scan the code below:

www.ingramcontent.com/pod-product-compliance
Lightning Source LLC
LaVergne TN
LVHW030630080426
835512LV00021B/3446